LIVING WORDS

WORDS

A LEGACY OF QUOTES

HELEN ROSEVEARE

It's not surprising that someone as memorable as Helen Roseveare should be so quotable. Her presence in Sydney in the early 80's helped shape a generation of gospel workers – my wife and I among them. But what is captured in these Living Words is Helen Roseveare's unique ability to be biblical, winsome, honest, warm-hearted, practical, compelling – all at once! She turns the gospel like a treasure in her hands, sharing her wonder at God's goodness in Christ. She fixes the reader with stare that asks, 'If God said it, then what are you and I going to do about it?' Helen Roseveare has the bearing of one refined by hardship, comforted by grace, embraced by God's people, resolute in seeing and sharing and obeying God's word. Her words seem to come off the page with a smile and a mischievous twinkle that says, 'You know, he's good for every one of his promises.'

Colin Buchanan
Christian Children's Recording artist and author, Sydney, Australia

LIVING WORDS

A LEGACY OF QUOTES

HELEN ROSEVEARE

CHRISTIAN
FOCUS

Copyright © Helen Roseveare 2019

paperback ISBN 978-1-5271-0295-8
epub ISBN 978-1-5271-0355-9
mobi ISBN 978-1-5271-0356-6

First published in 2019
by
Christian Focus Publications Ltd,
Geanies House, Fearn, Ross-shire,
IV20 1TW, Scotland, U.K.
www.christianfocus.com

Cover design & Typeset by Pete Barnsley (CreativeHoot.com)
Printed by Gutenberg, Malta

CONTENTS

INTRODUCTION

Helen Roseveare and I were close friends for nearly forty years. We knew that our friendship was a gracious gift from our loving Heavenly Father; so we did not regard it lightly but as something precious, given for our mutual support, encouragement, and strengthening in the Christian faith, but supremely given to be for the praise of His glory.

Helen and I first met at a Christian holiday camp for schoolgirls toward the end of the 1970s; Helen had been invited to this idyllic setting in the Scottish Highlands as a guest of the camp leadership to allow her time to continue convalescence from major surgery she had undergone only a very few weeks earlier. I too was at that camp, as a member of the leadership team in the role of camp medical officer. In addition to looking after any medical needs of the girls, I was asked to keep a careful eye on Helen, ensuring she had all necessary medications and anything else that would assist her recovery. And so in this setting of doctor and patient our long personal friendship was born! We found that right from our first meeting we 'clicked' discovering that we had many common interests – a love of nature and beautiful things in life, a deep respect for young people with a longing that each person should hear the good news of the Gospel, and not least a sense of humour – I was soon to discover that life with Helen would never be dull! Above all we shared our mutual love for our Saviour the Lord Jesus Christ and His Word; indeed our shared desire was to live in submission and loving obedience to His plan for each of our lives.

It will not be too surprising to the reader to learn that in the months following, Helen paid my mother and me two or three brief visits when she came to stay with us for the weekend. Indeed Helen often joked, when replying to questions about our friendship, 'I came with my suitcase for the weekend but stayed instead for forty years!'

At the time when our friendship began Helen's life had entered a period of testing and some uncertainty. She had only recently returned to the UK after twenty years of gruelling service in the Democratic Republic of Congo (DRC) and with no prospect of an early return she was seeking to know God's will for her future. 'Worldwide Evangelisation for Christ' (WEC), the missionary society of which Helen was a member, would soon rightly decree that she should not return to the DRC for at least five years because of the recent surgery. However, prior to this they had suggested that she might accept an invitation to visit the U.S.A. and undertake some speaking engagements on behalf of the mission to be organised by the American Headquarters. Helen accepted the invitation; the visit stretched to around 9 months and took her to many parts of that vast country, north, south, west and east; it proved to be a real blessing to many thousands of people across all age groups, occupations, ethnicities and church affiliations.

Helen had only been in America for about two weeks when sadly, she received news of her mother's unexpected death. Despite her grief, the tour continued without interruption; then seven months later, about six weeks from its end, Helen developed her own health problem which she knew would require urgent surgery; she said nothing to anyone about this, completed the programme, and then underwent major surgery straight after her return to the U.K.

It was no coincidence, when precisely at this time, God revealed His plan for the next phase of Helen's life, and in this our developing friendship would have an important part.

Within six months of leaving the U.S.A., invitations to return there and undertake further public ministry were starting to arrive, including one to speak at the biennial Student Conference in Urbana where thousands of Christian students gathered from all over America.

Helen now believed that a public-speaking ministry was indeed God's purpose for at least the next few years – and so with her 'eyes fixed on Jesus' she embarked on a 'race' that was to become one major part of the remarkable next phase of her life, one which would last well over thirty-five years.

In the light of these developments it was decided that Helen would make our home in Northern Ireland her U.K. hub, where she would return at the end of each period of ministry (usually about 6-8 weeks, sometimes longer) to take a well earned rest, recharge her batteries, and prepare for the next tour, often in another part of the world.

In order to give the reader a glimpse of the breadth of the public ministry she undertook, it may be worth mentioning that over the years Helen visited every area of the U.K. and Ireland, also Canada and America, multiple times; her worldwide speaking engagements included also, often more than once, visits to Australia and New Zealand, to Finland, Switzerland, Germany, Poland and Hungary, in Europe; a single trip to Mexico; in Asia she travelled to Singapore, Hong Kong and Afghanistan; she especially enjoyed two return visits to her beloved Nebobongo and Nyankunde, the centres of her twenty years of missionary service, in the DRC.

Helen's writing ministry, the second and perhaps more important part, of her working life during these forty years, was no less productive! Her first autobiography *Give me this Mountain* telling the story of the first 10 years in the Congo, including her capture during the Simba uprising, had been published in 1966; its sequel, *He gave us a Valley*, describes events she experienced in this devastated war-torn country in the immediate post-rebellion years after Belgium granted it independence. This book first appeared in 1980 around the start of her public ministry. Currently nine of Helen's works are in print, including her final book *Count it all Joy* published posthumously in 2017.

It might be of interest to the reader to learn that it was during the few short weeks between speaking engagements, (usually around 4-6) that Helen made the time to undertake most of her subsequent writing. She had an amazing capacity to 'switch off' from the present occupation in order to grasp any opportunity, however short, to get apart to write another few paragraphs or finish a chapter.

Between the years 1980 and 1992 the four 'living books' appeared and were initially published by Hodder and Stoughton. Their titles were derived from four foundational principles of WEC, sacrifice, faith, holiness and fellowship which the membership was expected to endorse. Helen, apparently, once suggested to the senior leadership of WEC rather casually, that perhaps it was time to rewrite these 'four pillars' as they were known for a new generation of 'Weccers'. The result – you have probably guessed – was the gift to a wider Christian world of *Living Sacrifice*, *Living Faith*, *Living Holiness* and *Living Fellowship*.

In my opinion, and I know that of others also, the 'living books' are amongst the *very best* of all Helen's writings. It was a great joy to her when after the publication of the third autobiography, *Digging Ditches,* in 2005, Christian Focus decided to reprint all the 'living series' also, and these appeared in their new format between 2006 and 2008. This meant that another generation of Christians could benefit from an enriched knowledge of the great doctrinal truths these books addressed, and *crucially* understanding of the doctrine demands its practical application to the individual's life; thus, with the help of the indwelling Holy Spirit, a gradual transformation nearer to the likeness of Jesus will take place; a life-changer that our heavenly Father had always purposed should become a 'living reality' brought about in the life of every one of His children, solely because of the Gospel.

In this new book *Living Words* Carine Mackenzie has given us a lovely gift, another 'jewel in the crown', and another opportunity to make the 'living books' more widely known and appreciated. *Living Words* is primarily a devotional book; it challenges us to repent of the paucity of our personal response to the Gospel which rightly demands the dedication of everything we are and have to the Lord Jesus Christ. As C. T. Studd, the founder of WEC, has famously stated: 'If Jesus Christ be God and died for me, then no sacrifice can be too great for me to make for Him'.

I loved re-reading *Living Sacrifice, Living Faith, Living Holiness* and *Living Fellowship* in this new presentation. It helped me to appreciate these glorious truths which we can so easily take for granted and to meditate in awesome wonder at the sheer vastness of the breadth and depth of the Salvation procured for us, but at what cost!

The Bible verse at the end of each chosen paragraph is another 'precious jewel' the book gives us, as it confirms that Helen's human words, though fallible, are indeed consistent with God's eternal infallible Truth. Much more importantly the Bible verse quoted exposes our minds and wills to the 'living Word' to do its own work in hearts and lives. As the Scripture says 'The Word of God is living and active, sharper than any two-edged sword ... discerning the thoughts and intentions of the heart' (Heb. 4: 12, ESV).

Helen went to be forever with her beloved Lord and Master in December 2016; today she is alive and rejoicing in His nearer Presence where she longed to be. Among the many tributes paid to her, reference often was made to Abel as he is mentioned in the list of heroes of the faith by the writer to the Hebrews: 'And by faith Abel still speaks, even though he is dead' (Heb. 11:4). Helen Roseveare still speaks today, and she will continue to do so because of the example of the inspirational life she lived, poured out in love and costly service to King Jesus; she speaks today also through her published works, as this book *Living Words* so clearly demonstrates, by the words that she wrote.

Pat Morton
September 2018

SOLI DEO GLORIA –
TO GOD ALONE BE THE GLORY.

LIVING
HOLINESS

But as I studied, I began to realise that love, like all the other attributes of God, is part of the greatest attribute of all, the HOLINESS of God.

'God is holy.'

This fact shines out of every page of the Scriptures, brilliant as the midday sun. It begins to blind one to all the other factors. Just as the sun's light is broken down by a raindrop into the separate colours of the spectrum, so the HOLINESS of God is broken down, so to speak, into the many-coloured spectrum of all His attributes – His goodness and mercy, His loving-kindness and forbearance, His righteousness and justice, His truth and wrath – so that we can see and understand what makes up this HOLINESS.

> *Be holy because*
> *I, the LORD your God, am holy.*
>
> LEVITICUS 19:2

No one told me that this longing in my heart was the work of the Holy Spirit and the beginning of what is called 'sanctification' – the process of making me holy, like unto the Lord Jesus. In fact, no one told me that this sanctifying work of the Spirit in my heart was the essential proof that He had regenerated my life. As soon as one is justified and saved, the work of sanctification must begin, and it is the Holy Spirit Himself who causes one to 'hunger after righteousness', to want to be good, as He makes real in one's heart that which God sees to be good; and to want to cease to be bad, as He shows one those things that displease God.

No. I did not understand that then; but I just knew, with a deep inner consciousness, that there must BE a goal to which my whole Christian life should be directed. Even though I hardly knew the word, let alone what it meant, I sensed that the goal was HOLINESS. So it came about that after the overwhelming joy of realising that my sins had been forgiven, I started out on a long quest after HOLINESS.

But we ought always to thank God for you, brothers loved by the Lord, because from the beginning God chose you to be saved through the sanctifying work of the Spirit and through belief in the truth.

2 THESSALONIANS 2:13

We constantly need to 'add to…' if we are to grow. He stresses that, far from being negligent in doing this, we should remember His teaching, that we might be stirred up to even greater endeavour.

'Add to…' That phrase kept coming back to me. It was a simple, straightforward thought. I was reasonably good at mathematics, and understood the basic concept of addition.

Then, two days later, I came to another phrase: 'grow in the grace and knowledge of our Lord and Saviour Jesus Christ' (2 Pet. 3:18). Equally, I knew enough about biology to understand the concept of growth!

Addition and growth. Physical and biological. The two concepts, taking root in my heart within one month of becoming a Christian, were to be the first stepping stones in my search for HOLINESS. I spent all the time I could, mornings and evenings, studying the Bible, 'soaking up', like the proverbial sponge, the Word of God. It excited me and challenged me, convinced me and stirred me. Every day I sought to 'add to' my knowledge and understanding of God and to 'grow in' grace and in the outworking of Scriptural principles in daily conduct.

For this very reason, make every effort to add to your faith goodness; and to goodness, knowledge.

2 PETER 1:5

Is it that we Christians today have an inadequate understanding of God's HOLINESS and therefore of His wrath against sin and of the awfulness of a Christless eternity? If we were gripped by two facts – of the necessity for judgment of sin because God is holy; and of the necessity of HOLINESS in the Christian that he may represent such a God to others – would we not 'hunger and thirst after righteousness' whatever the cost, and would not others then see Christ in us, and be drawn to Him?

In other words, if we were to rightly present the Scriptural teaching on the need of HOLINESS in the life of every believer, we should not need to plead for missionaries. Would the former not result in the latter?

Blessed are those who hunger and thirst for righteousness, for they will be filled.

MATTHEW 5:6

If we have begun to appreciate the awful sinfulness of sin, and that the only way a holy God could save us from its guilt and penalty was by the death – the actual, physical, brutal death – of His only Son, we would realise *from what* He had redeemed us. Understanding this, would we not then understand *for what* He had redeemed us – for unremitting service, as His ambassadors, telling others, while it is yet the day of grace, of the wonderful news of Christ's death for sinners?

If we are to fulfil this purpose for which we are saved, not only must the emphasis be on the *fact* of HOLINESS as seen in Christ, but also on the essential *need* of HOLINESS in our lives that we may properly reveal Christ to others.

A testimony to salvation without a resultant HOLINESS of character and conduct is a contradiction. It is, as St James says, a dead faith, if it has not the witness of works.

With all my heart, I endorse the fact that we are not, and never can be, saved by good works; we are saved and redeemed because Christ died on the Cross of Calvary in our place, becoming our sin, our great Substitute:

Bearing scorn and scoffing rude
In my place condemned He stood.

We are saved as the result of Redemption, wrought for us by our Saviour alone. We are no longer our own. We have been bought at a price, the price of His shed blood. We are now His, our bodies indwelt by the risen Saviour through the ministry of the Holy Spirit. He, working in us and through us, will do the 'yet greater works' that He promised, and our faith, which has brought us to know and acknowledge our Redeemer, will reveal itself alive and active by the fruit that is seen in our character, and the acts that transform our conduct.

By their fruit you will recognise them (Matt. 7:20).

I tell you the truth, anyone who has faith in me will do what I have been doing. He will do even greater things than these, because I am going to the Father.

JOHN 14:12

'But the day of the Lord will come like a thief,' [Peter says in 2 Peter 3:10-12]. 'The heavens will disappear with a roar; the elements will be destroyed by fire, and the earth and everything in it will be laid bare.

Since everything will be destroyed in this way, what kind of people ought you to be? You ought to live holy and godly lives as you look forward to the Day of God and speed its coming.'

Listen also to the words of the apostle John, in his letter to the scattered Christians of his day, many of whom were already suffering persecution under the Roman empire: 'continue in him, so that when he appears we may be confident and unashamed before him at his coming' (1 John 2:28).

So then, just as you received Christ Jesus as Lord, continue to live your lives in him.

COLOSSIANS 2:6

The apostle John is very clear about the essential characteristic of a Christian: 'no one who lives in Christ keeps on sinning', and again: 'no one who is born of God will continue to sin (habitually).' He is not saying that it is impossible for a Christian to sin. What he is saying is that it is impossible for a Christian both to abide in Christ and to continue in habitual, deliberate sin. The heretics of his day either presumed a blindness to sin, saying it was not there, or were merely indifferent to it, saying that it did not matter. These are still the devil's tactics, as he endeavours to blind our eyes to the total incongruity of 'continuing in sin' once we have been redeemed by the precious blood of Christ.

> *No one who lives in him keeps on sinning.*
> *No one who continues to sin has either seen*
> *him or known him.*
>
> 1 JOHN 3:6

On each occasion, the Holy Spirit started His work in the heart of someone by convicting him of sin, leading him to godly repentance and, as far as possible, to restitution. As each forgiven and restored sinner came to realise something more of what Christ had done for him at Calvary, the love of God flooded over him, filling his heart with a desire to know God's Word and to search out His commands, that he might obey them. By the grace of God, this way of obedience developed in the believer a truly Christlike desire to serve others. 'The Son of Man did not come to be served, but to serve, and to give his life as a ransom for many' (Matt. 20:28).

When Christ washed the disciples' feet in the upper room, the evening before He was crucified, He told them to serve one another as He had served them.

Now that I, your Lord and Teacher, have washed your feet, you also should wash one another's feet. I have set you an example that you should do as I have done for you.

JOHN 13:14-15

The Holy Spirit desires to work in me the grace of repentance, purifying and cleansing me as I deliberately mortify and put away sinful practices.

He then pours into my heart the love of God, causing me to be able to love God truly and sincerely, with no ulterior motives, no subtle self-pleasing or self-gratification.

This love will reveal itself by an ever-increasing desire to obey God in every smallest detail, as the Holy Spirit prompts me through the reading of the Scriptures.

And this obedience will result in untiring service to my fellow men, to the glory of God, untarnished by any thought of what I personally will 'get out of it'.

This is the ministry of the Holy Spirit to bring about 'living HOLINESS' in the life of every Christian believer.

Just as you used to offer yourselves as slaves to impurity and to ever-increasing wickedness, so now offer yourselves as slaves to righteousness leading to holiness.

ROMANS 6:19

We have to be convinced of sin in our lives, and that this sin is 'dirt' in the eyes of a holy God, whose 'eyes are too pure to look on evil,' and who 'cannot tolerate wrong' (Hab. 1:13). This conviction of sin should lead us to repentance and true sorrow for that which grieves God; a godly repentance which, in turn, should lead us to a deliberate intention to forsake the sin and be done with it, to turn '*from* idols *to* … God' (1 Thess. 1:9).

Sadly, one has to acknowledge that we can so confess and make restitution for our sin in order to 'feel good', with no heart involvement and no realisation that our sin has grieved the heart of the God who loves us.

Jesus wants His children to show true repentance. His first message was: 'Repent, for the kingdom of heaven is near' (Matt. 4:17), and one of His final instructions to His disciples before His ascension was that they should preach 'repentance and forgiveness of sins … in his Name' (Luke 24:47) everywhere, to all men.

Therefore, since we have these promises, dear friends, let us purify ourselves from everything that contaminates body and spirit, perfecting holiness out of reverence for God.

2 CORINTHIANS 7:1

As we see God as the Potter and ourselves as the clay in His hands ready to be moulded into the pattern that He has already planned, ready for the job He has purposed, it is easy to understand that the grit or gravel represents the sin in our lives that spoils the design. The finer the walls of the clay vessel become, the more clearly will a speck of grit be seen.

Godly repentance is the willingness to allow the Master Potter to extrude that grit. It is the birth of the desire to turn away from all that is not holy, and must be the first step towards HOLINESS.

God cannot allow sin to remain in the lives of His children. The 'vase' He is making would be marred, and that is inconceivable. No, indeed! Sin must be cast out, and for this God must work into the heart of each believer a realisation of the sinfulness of sin, from which it cost the very Son of God His life-blood to redeem us. In turn, as we realise the sinfulness of sin, the Holy Spirit can give us a growing hatred for that sin which crucified the Saviour.

Yet you, LORD, are our Father. We are the clay, you are the potter; we are all the work of your hand.

ISAIAH 64:8

Always, in revivals, the Holy Spirit creates in the hearts of Christians a hatred of sin, not just of its consequences. The Ten Commandments take on a new role in their lives, revealing God's standards for Christlike conduct. Coupled with Christ's own words in the sermon given on the mount (Matt. 5–7), the Christians begin to allow the Holy Spirit to compare their individual lives with the pattern given in Scripture, and conviction of sin grows. People see anger and irritation as sin. Wrong desires and covetous jealousy are seen to be sin. Discontent, grumbling, unbelief, wanting one's own way, all manifestations of self and pride, are recognised as they truly are – *sin*.

The Potter is at work, removing the gravel that mars the vessel.

How much more, then, will the blood of Christ, who through the eternal Spirit offered himself unblemished to God, cleanse our consciences from acts that lead to death, so that we may serve the living God!

HEBREWS 9:14

During seasons of revival, Christians come under deep conviction by the Holy Spirit and the awful revelation of the pain that our sins cause our Saviour. The quick retort of self-vindication, the subtle use of words to say one thing yet mean another, the nursed hurt despite the outward shaking of hands, the easy excuse that 'everybody else does it, so what?', the plausible reasoning to make wrong look right – all these are seen to be *sin*.

The Potter is still at work, now removing the finest grit that mars His planned vessel.

It is God Himself who reveals sin to be sin. It is the Holy Spirit in my heart that causes me to be 'uncomfortable' about that which He wishes to show me is wrong. I have found that I do not have to search my heart to seek out wrong things. They become clearly wrong to me as I open my heart to the influence of the Spirit.

Once anyone begins to sense that some action or thought or desire in their lives is wrong (that is, wrong for them), it is useless to argue about it, or discuss it with others, or seek to excuse it by circumstances, custom or culture. It just has to go, or one has no peace.

One also finds that one does not necessarily come under condemnation by hearing someone else's confession of sin. It could be that what one confesses does not yet bring another under conviction for the same act. The Spirit moves in each heart, revealing and convicting as each one is ready to receive and respond. He becomes to us like a wonderful 'private tutor', a school master who cares for each of His pupils individually, and is willing to give infinite time to the training and perfecting of each life given into His care.

If my people, who are called by my name, will humble themselves and pray and seek my face and turn from their wicked ways, then I will hear from heaven, and I will forgive their sin and will heal their land.

2 CHRONICLES 7:14

When one is first converted and one's name is written in the Lamb's Book of Life, one is proud to wear the uniform ('clothe yourselves with the Lord Jesus Christ', Rom. 13:14), and the badge ('you were marked in him with a seal', Eph. 1:13), but one has not yet received the diploma ('Holy to the Lord', Exod. 39:30). The potential, the promise, the purpose are all clear, but the practical outworking in the daily life has yet to be experienced.

From the start, the unlearning of the wrong already imparted by the previous teacher is as difficult as the understanding and absorbing of the new material being taught. The first week in the Christian life may seem one great shattering failure, our conscience many times each day convicting us of transgressing the new rules and of missing the mark in the new studies. The devil whispers in our ears that we are not converted at all! He laughs at us that we could even think we were. He taunts us with our failures, saying that these prove we are still in *his* school.

Be self-controlled and alert. Your enemy the devil prowls around like a roaring lion looking for someone to devour. Resist him, standing firm in the faith, because you know that your brothers throughout the world are undergoing the same kind of sufferings.

1 PETER 5:8-9

So it is only the Holy Spirit who can make us want to be holy, revealing what things are sin (conviction) and giving us a hatred for these things and a great desire to be rid of them (true repentance). As I grew up, I had only hated the consequence of sin; as I sought to go on with God, however, I had a growing hatred of sin itself.

Then an urge began to grow in me to put right all I could of the wrong that I had inflicted on others – restoring what was stolen, confessing to what was untrue, forgiving where I had borne a grudge, loving where before I had felt hatred. This 'putting right' of wrongs committed can never merit or earn forgiveness, any more than we can gain salvation by good works: but it is the outcome of a contrite heart. As the Holy Spirit convinced us of sin, and grants to us godly repentance, so also He brings to birth in us this desire to make restitution.

Bear with each other and forgive one another if any of you has a grievance against someone. Forgive as the Lord forgave you.

COLOSSIANS 3:13

There are times when there is nothing we can do to repair the damage we have caused, yet it is still true that a 'broken and contrite heart, O God, You will not despise' (Ps. 51:17, ESV). His forgiveness is dependent only on the finished work at Calvary. Spirit-given repentance only brings about my personal identification with the redeeming grace of God – nothing else. As the Spirit of God works in me that 'broken and contrite heart', I shall seek to express it by 'fruit in keeping with repentance' (Matt. 3:8; Luke 3:8), deliberate turning from sin, resolute seeking by God's grace to be done with the hateful thing that caused me to fail, and where possible, reparation for the past.

Whether there is a *crisis* start to this life of 'being made holy as He is holy' or not; whether there is a date when one first agrees with God's verdict on one's life and of one's need of the ministry of the Holy Spirit in sanctifying grace, or not, there *must be a continuance*, a daily dying to self, an hourly 'being filled' with the Spirit. When Paul declared, 'I have been crucified with Christ and I no longer live, but Christ lives in me,' the Greek words, I believe, could equally well be translated: 'I am being crucified with Christ … so that Christ may continually be living in me' (Gal. 2:20).

> *Godly sorrow brings repentance that leads to salvation and leaves no regret, but worldly sorrow brings death.*
>
> 2 CORINTHIANS 7:10

That he *loves* God – isn't this, surely, the immediate positive sign in the heart of a new believer, that the Holy Spirit has indeed brought him into the state of regeneration? As the Spirit convinces us of sin and leads us to repentance, so also He pours out into our hearts (Rom. 5:5) the LOVE of God. This is the work of Christ on our behalf because He loved us:

> *This is how we know what love is: Jesus Christ laid down his life for us* (1 John 3:16).

> *The Son of God, who loved me and gave himself for me* (Gal. 2:20).

> *This is how God showed his love among us: he sent his one and only Son into the world that we might live through him* (1 John 4:9).

And we find ourselves loving Him:

> *We love [Him] because he first loved us* (1 John 4:19).

We have naturally no such love toward God in our hearts. On the contrary, before entering into our new relationship as God's children by adoption, we tend to hate all that is good and holy and of God, because our natural man is rebuked and made to feel uncomfortable in the presence of His HOLINESS. When, however, we become members of God's family, the Holy Spirit pours into our hearts the very love of God, and we find ourselves loving Him with His love.

> **For God so loved the world that he gave his one and only Son, that whoever believes in him shall not perish but have eternal life.**
> JOHN 3:16

This love is holy, and pure, and altogether good. It may be almost without emotional content, because it is beyond the concepts of human emotion. It is not sentimental, nor superficial; it absorbs our whole being. This new power of love finds expression, firstly in a previously unknown desire to worship God Himself, and then, secondly, in outreach to all around us. Jesus Himself told us that this would be *the* way that others would know the reality of our new experience of salvation: 'A new command I give you: Love one another. As I have loved you, so you must love one another. By this all men will know that you are my disciples, if you love one another' (John 13:34-35).

Dear friends, let us love one another, for love comes from God. Everyone who loves has been born of God and knows God.

1 JOHN 4:7

Christ gives us that new commandment (in John 13:34-35) at the end of a very dramatic chapter, in which He shows us clearly two levels in which we can express this new divine love to one another. He was actually teaching His disciples some very deep and discerning lessons in leadership, lessons that are entirely different from the usual worldly ones on the same subject. In the world, a leader is a Somebody, somebody before whom the world around bows down and to whom they show utmost respect.

Dear friends, since God so loved us,
we also ought to love one another.

1 JOHN 4:11

God's way for Christian leaders (and all of us) is so different. In the world's estimation, it is a way 'down' rather than 'up'. At the supper table in the upper room, when Jesus partook of the feast of the Passover with His disciples, He, the very Son of God, 'took off his outer clothing, and wrapped a towel round his waist' in order to pour water into a basin, and knelt and washed the disciples' dusty feet. He did the most menial task, that not one of His disciples had been willing to undertake, a task usually performed by the lowest of the slaves, someone on the bottom rung of the so-called social ladder. Our Lord did it willingly, naturally, and with no loss to His dignity or His authority – because He loved them. 'You call me "Teacher" and "Lord", and rightly so, for that is what I am. Now that I, your Lord and Teacher, have washed your feet, you also should wash one another's feet' (John 13:13, 14). Christ showed that true spiritual leadership is revealed in servanthood.

Instead, whoever wants to become great among you must be your servant.

MARK 10:43

The more we seek to understand 'the incomparable riches' of the Grace of God, who planned our redemption from before the foundation of the world, because of His 'great love for us', the more conscious we become of the shallowness of our love for Him. That we ought to love Him, as we consider all He has done for us through His death on the Cross as propitiation for our sins, we are never in doubt; but whether we do love Him, in actual daily fact and experience, we may well begin to question. A deep yearning in our innermost being 'to know Him more clearly, love Him more dearly and follow Him more nearly' is probably all to which we dare lay claim. Those who have such feelings are, as A.W. Tozer so aptly puts it in *The Pursuit of God* (published by Oliphants), 'athirst to taste for themselves the piercing sweetness of the love of Christ.'

As the Psalmist puts it in Psalm 42:1-2:

As the deer pants for streams of water,
So my soul pants for you, O God.
My soul thirsts for God, for the living God.

> **In him we have redemption through his blood,**
> **the forgiveness of sins, in accordance with the**
> **riches of God's grace.**
>
> EPHESIANS 1:7

Christ loved me enough to die for me while I was yet His enemy. If God had waited for me to learn to love Him before He died, I would never have been saved. I knew that with my head, but when I met someone who behaved in such a completely Christlike way, I was amazed. In the twenty years of my life in Congo/Zaire, Tamoma's love for me only grew deeper and stronger. Her home was always open to me, her friendship was unchanging. When I found myself spiritually discouraged or physically overtired, the obvious place to turn for love and comfort, be it also for rebuke and teaching, was Adzangwe, the village of Pastor Ndugu and his wife; and they were always available to God to channel to me that which I needed.

For if, while we were God's enemies, we were reconciled to him through the death of his Son, how much more, having been reconciled, shall we be saved through his life!

ROMANS 5:10

The sadness of today's prevalent attitude in so many situations – 'what do I get out of it?' – is in stark contrast to the attitude of love stirred by the Holy Spirit in a believer's heart – 'what can I give to help in this situation?'

'God so loved the world that He gave …' no end, no time limit, no measure, no calculation. His giving could only be called a reckless abandonment of love. Do I love Him in like measure, and am I willing to show it by a similar reckless abandonment? Even though others may call the giving up of my rights to my own selfish ambitions sacrifice, do I believe that it is in fact only privilege?

Am I willing… to give up time or sleep or watching a television programme or going to a football match, for example, to do some small service to another in need, just because I love my Saviour? Am I willing … to give up a high salary or prospects of promotion, and my own private ambitions, in order, for example, to go and serve others in some needy corner of the mission fields of the world, or to supply what is needed to enable someone else to go? Love, as an expression of HOLINESS, will stir such 'giving' in my life.

Give, and it will be given to you. A good measure, pressed down, shaken together and running over, will be poured into your lap. For with the measure you use, it will be measured to you.

LUKE 6:38

God gave us the Ten Commandments, to assist us to develop habits in our new Christian lives compatible with His HOLINESS. These rules have been likened to the 'blinkers' on a horse running in a race, which prevent him from being distracted by movements on the sidelines and encourage him to keep looking straight ahead. Christ increased the dynamism of this godly 'rule of life' by insisting that it applies to that which motivates us as well as to our overt actions. Not for one minute did He allow us to think that by the new Covenant in His blood were the old Covenant rules abrogated. No, indeed! Those Ten Commandments provide clear, practical rules for daily living, and I must 'leave behind' any habits from my old life that are inconsistent with His standard for holy living. I am not more free to choose the rules for such holy living, when I enter God's family, than a football player is free to make his own rules for play, when he is invited to become a member of his county team! Do I love my God enough to say 'Yes!' to His rules, even when this means saying 'No' to my own desires?

Those who live according to the sinful nature have their minds set on what that nature desires; but those who live in accordance with the Spirit have their minds set on what the Spirit desires.

ROMANS 8:5

This attitude of heart and mind, that can joyfully trust God in all circumstances, can only take possession of me as I allow the Holy Spirit to fill me with love for my Lord. The promise is to 'those who love Him'. Let us remind ourselves that we only love Him because He first loved us and because He has poured His own love into our hearts in order that we have wherewith to love Him. When this amazing love of God takes over and controls my life, I can truly accept 'all things' from His hands without murmuring or dispute.

And hope does not disappoint us, because God has poured out his love into our hearts by the Holy Spirit, whom he has given us.

ROMANS 5:5

God longs, above all, for us to bring Him our love. It is by obedience to His first great commandment: 'Love the LORD your God with all your heart and with all your soul and with all your strength' (Deut. 6:5) and also to His new commandment: 'Love one another. As I have loved you, so you must love one another' (John 13:34) that we witness to others that we are Christians. 'All men will know that you are my disciples if you love one another,' is His Word to us. This 'love' is to be self-giving involvement for the good of others rather than ourselves, caring for them and serving them. 'As I have loved you,' said our Lord, was to be the model of our loving.

> *He answered, 'Love the Lord your God with all your heart and with all your soul and with all your strength and with all your mind'; and, 'Love your neighbour as yourself.'*
>
> LUKE 10:27

Are we not in danger of turning all this upside down? Have we lost sight of God's purpose for our life that it might be one of self-*giving* love? Have we not become overwhelmingly selfish, seeking to 'get' rather than to 'give'? The contrast between God's plan and our practice is almost unbelievable. To right this wrong, God *gave* Himself for us at Calvary. The holy Lamb of God, without spot or blemish, died in our place, as our Substitute. God longs for the response of our hearts, that we should seek Him first and His righteousness, *giving* Him His rightful place in our lives, putting Him first in everything and crowning Him King, not just in hymnody, but in reality.

As the Holy Spirit continues to work in our hearts and lives, transforming us into conformity to the image of God's Son, not only will He burn up the sin and dross in our lives, but He will create in us an intense longing to *give* God all we are and have, because 'we so love Him who first loved us.'

But seek first his kingdom and his righteousness, and all these things will be given to you as well.

MATTHEW 6:33

God's HOLINESS is like a consuming fire. Not only will it burn up all the dross and impurities in our lives – the impatience, pride, anger – leading us to true godly repentance, but also it will melt the stony and soften the hard in our lives – the self-seeking, the self-vindicating, the self-righteousness – filling us with true godly love. I need to pray: 'Spirit of the living God … melt *me*!'

We can use hardness of heart as a defence mechanism, protecting us from becoming too involved in another's pain. It can enable us to remain outside situations without being hurt by them, even when we give an appearance of being involved, but such hardness and stony-heartedness can keep others at arms' length.

> *I will give you a new heart and put a new spirit in you; I will remove from you your heart of stone and give you a heart of flesh.*
>
> EZEKIEL 36:26

The Holy Spirit, in His gracious work of sanctification in our hearts, gives us certain specific gifts that we may be holy and pleasing to God in our daily lives. Firstly, He gives us the gift of conviction of sin, and with it the ability to repent. Secondly, He pours into our hearts the love of God, thus enabling us to love God and our fellow men. Thirdly, He gives us the desire to obey God's Word and commandments, and the ability to do so, *with enjoyment*, in the little as in the bigger things of daily life.

Fourthly, the Holy Spirit gives us the privilege of realising that we are God's servants, chosen to be His ambassadors in this world in which we live, and He then gives us the ability to undertake that service in a manner wholly pleasing to God.

There is a temptation in the Church today to short-circuit the work of the Holy Spirit, and try to go from step two to step four, without bothering about step three. I am well aware that we cannot actually divide up our lives like that, into neat compartments, and that these four 'steps' are continuous, and overlap each other with no fixed borders. Perhaps these 'steps' are rather like the hoofs of a galloping horse, where all four are essential, repeatedly essential, until the race is finished, and it is often practically impossible to see the order in which they move!

> *Therefore, there is now no condemnation for those who are in Christ Jesus, because through Christ Jesus the law of the Spirit who gives life has set you free from the law of sin and death.*
>
> ROMANS 8:1-2

Christ Himself never ceased to tell His disciples throughout His three years of public ministry that He was always activated by the desire to *obey* His Father and to fulfil His Father's will. Even when that obedience meant going to His death at Calvary, we can overhear Him say in prayer to His Father, in the Garden of Gethsemane, 'Yet not as I will, but as you will' (Matt. 26:39).

Paul underlines this, when he stresses that we are to have the same mind as our Saviour: 'He humbled himself and became obedient to death – even death on a cross' (Phil. 2:8).

In other words, all we do in God's service should stem from our earnest desire to *obey* Him, rather than only from a desire to show Him that we love Him. The two may often appear to be the same, but we do well to make firm the foundation on which we build our endeavours towards HOLINESS.

> And this is love: that we walk in obedience to his commands. As you have heard from the beginning, his command is that you walk in love.
>
> 2 JOHN 6

When I first started Bible reading, under the guidance of the Scripture Union notes, I well remember that we were encouraged to 'look for an example to follow, a warning to heed, a command to obey' every day, so that our study would not be merely a case of gathering knowledge in our heads, but be translated into practical wisdom to help us to know how to live.

James exhorts us to be 'doers of the Word' and 'not hearers only': 'Do not merely listen to the Word,' he writes, 'and so deceive yourselves. Do what it says' (James 1:22). In fact, James goes on to liken the person who reads and promptly forgets or ignores the practical implications of what he has read, to some short-sighted person who glances in a mirror, and immediately forgets what he looks like!

> *He replied, 'Blessed rather are those who hear the word of God and obey it.'*
>
> LUKE 11:28

What about commands with regard to our use of time? Does the Bible give us any definite guidance here? Notice what is said in Ephesians 5:15-21: 'Be very careful, then, how you live – not as unwise but as wise, making the most of every opportunity… be filled with the Spirit… always giving thanks to God the Father for everything…' Do I actually consider *all* my time to be important in God's service? Do I *seek* to use every opportunity to represent God's interests in the company of those around me? Am I *always* full of gratitude to God, whatever the circumstances?

Rejoice always, pray continually, give thanks in all circumstances; for this is God's will for you in Christ Jesus.

1 THESSALONIANS 5:16-18

How do we react to the command given us in 1 Thessalonians 5:16-18? 'Be joyful always; pray continually; give thanks in all circumstances, for this is God's will for you in Christ Jesus.'

Is it actually possible to be joyful always, even when everything seems to be going wrong? Can one pray continually, even in the midst of overwhelming pressures? Can one sincerely thank God in the midst of crushing sorrow?

Jesus 'for the joy set before Him endured the Cross,' and He can fill me with His joy at all times. If I maintain a close relationship with my Lord, and seek always to do only those things that please Him, I can pray in the midst of any situation. Whatever sorrow seeks to shatter me, I can thank God for trusting me with the experience even if I cannot understand the reason for it.

For his anger lasts only a moment, but his favor lasts a lifetime; weeping may stay for the night, but rejoicing comes in the morning.

PSALM 30:5

Christ warns us again and again that worldly riches, which probably include not only money and possessions, but also public opinion and popularity, can so easily take over and dominate our lives to the exclusion of everything else.

He explained the meaning of the parable of the sower thus: 'What was sown among the thorns is the man who hears the Word, but the worries of this life and the deceitfulness of wealth choke it, making it unfruitful' (see Matt. 13:22).

Are we willing to be warned about our attitude to worldly wealth, and to keep 'things' in perspective? Is my spiritual life and its development more important than the acquisition of possessions, material and abstract?

Jesus answered, 'If you want to be perfect, go, sell your possessions and give to the poor, and you will have treasure in heaven. Then come, follow me.'

MATTHEW 19:21

The spiritual process of learning obedience is frequently closely associated with *suffering* in one form or another. This 'suffering' may be only anticipatory, because the very word 'obedience' can conjure up today the idea of submission to another who wishes to dominate. Therefore the one giving the obedience is tempted to think that he will automatically have to give up his rights to self-expression, and so 'suffer' the indignity of servitude. On the other hand, the 'suffering' may be the means needed to help someone to realise that only by obedience can the reality of their love and respect for another be shown. The suffering may be physical, but more probably it will be mental or emotional, as one learns to exchange a desire to dominate for a desire to serve.

As Christians, the close link between obedience and suffering should not surprise us when we remember: 'Although he was a Son, he learned obedience through what he suffered' (Heb. 5:8, ESV).

Dear friends, do not be surprised at the painful trial you are suffering, as though something strange were happening to you. But rejoice that you participate in the sufferings of Christ, so that you may be overjoyed when his glory is revealed.

1 PETER 4:12-13

Hatred of sin and love for the Saviour must lead, first and foremost, to obedience. Obedience to the Word of God will show itself in service. Because I love Him, I delight to obey Him; because I obey Him, I delight to serve Him. This will be true godly service, a giving without any thought of gaining.

> *I beseech you, therefore, brethren, by the mercies of God, that ye present your bodies a living sacrifice, holy, acceptable unto God, which is your reasonable service. And be not conformed to this world: but be ye transformed by the renewing of your mind, that ye may prove what is that good, and acceptable, and perfect, will of God'.* (Rom. 12:1, 2, KJV)

'Reasonable service' is translated in newer versions as 'spiritual worship'. To be acceptable to God, both service and worship must be holy and in obedience to His command that we should offer ourselves as 'living sacrifices'. Christ died on the Cross as our vicarious sacrifice. Not only must there have been a decisive act in the past when I committed my life to Christ, being identified with Him in His death, but there must also be a continual daily identifying of myself with that death, in putting aside my own will and self-pleasing, in order to live according to His will and good pleasure.

With all wisdom and understanding, he made known to us the mystery of his will according to his good pleasure, which he purposed in Christ.

EPHESIANS 1:8-9

'The life I live in the body, I live by faith in the Son of God, who loved me and gave himself for me' (Gal. 2:20).

The writer to the Hebrews says, 'Let us have grace, whereby we may serve God acceptably with reverence and godly fear: for our God is a consuming fire' (Heb. 12:28, 29, KJV). Expounding this verse, the New Bible Commentary puts it very clearly: 'Let us appropriate the grace so abundantly available to serve God and in the face of such a prospect this will be with a real sense of unworthiness and awe. Only those who thus follow after HOLINESS will survive his judgment, see the Lord, and reign eternally with him.'

Here is a trustworthy saying: If we died with him, we will also live with him; if we endure, we will also reign with him. If we disown him, he will also disown us; if we are faithless, he remains faithful, for he cannot disown himself.

2 TIMOTHY 2:11-13

To *act justly* is the way that God has planned for us to live, in order to achieve His purpose and to fulfil His will. It is the appointed way to 'serve God acceptably', and to show forth the HOLINESS that the Spirit is creating in us.

This HOLINESS will reveal itself also in a God-given desire to *love mercy*. We shall seek always to lift those who are down, to encourage those who are discouraged, to help those in need. We shall be willing to think the best of another, rather than the worst; to be grieved when another fails, rather than to rejoice in his downfall; to pray rather than to gossip.

This HOLINESS will enable us to *'walk humbly'* with our God – to walk humbly with God we need to be transformed into His image by the Holy Spirit and this is achieved by deliberate obedience to all He reveals to us. We must give Him *all* that we are and have. There has to be a *total* surrender and *absolute* submission of our will to His, a true echoing of the prayer of the Saviour in the Garden of Gethsemane: 'Not as I will, but as you will' (Matt. 26:39).

He has shown you, O mortal, what is good. And what does the LORD require of you? To act justly and to love mercy and to walk humbly with your God.

MICAH 6:8

When, in prayer, we look at ourselves honestly and recognise our poverty of spiritual experience; our stunted growth and continuing immaturity; our lack of love and devotion to God and to our fellow men; our spirit of grumbling and discontent; our quickness to criticise others, we shall marvel that God has called us to be co-labourers with Him. Only then shall we walk humbly with our God, awed by His gracious patience and long-suffering forbearance.

'Acting justly' as Christ would, in each circumstance, and so revealing Christlikeness to others in all we do and how we do it: 'loving mercy' and yearning over the welfare of suffering humanity around us, seeking by all means to bring them to Christ: 'walking humbly' before God who has called us out of darkness into His marvellous light; this is HOLINESS, revealing itself in service.

But you are a chosen people, a royal priesthood, a holy nation, God's special possession, that you may declare the praises of him who called you out of darkness into his wonderful light.

1 PETER 2:9

Outward HOLINESS is revealed by the Holy Spirit in the life of the Christian, through the manifesting of the nine-fold fruit – love, joy, peace, patience, kindness, goodness, faithfulness, gentleness and self-control – in service to others. This HOLINESS of conduct is channelled into the good works that God has fore-ordained for each one of us: 'For we are God's workmanship, created in Christ Jesus to do good works, which God prepared in advance for us to do' (Eph. 2:10). These good works are like the fragrance that filled the house when Mary broke the alabaster box, in order to pour out all the very costly ointment, to anoint the feet of our Lord Jesus Christ. He said that what she had done was 'a good work, a beautiful thing.'

But the fruit of the Spirit is love, joy, peace, patience, kindness, goodness, faithfulness, gentleness and self-control. Against such things there is no law. Those who belong to Christ Jesus have crucified the sinful nature with its passions and desires.

GALATIANS 5:22-24

Such service has to know the 'must' of *obedience to love's compulsion*. All His life, Christ had this *must* upon Him.

As a twelve-year-old, in Jerusalem after the feast of the Passover, He said to His parents, 'Didn't you know I had to be in my Father's house?' (Luke 2:49).

On His way from Jerusalem to Galilee, during His three years of ministry, it is said: 'Now he (Jesus) had to go through Samaria' (John 4:4) – just to meet a needy woman, drawing water at the well.

As He went to the Garden of Gethsemane on that fateful last evening before Calvary, our Lord said to His disciples, 'It is written: "And he was numbered with the transgressors"; and I tell you that this must be fulfilled in me' (Luke 22:37).

It is the LORD your God you must follow, and him you must revere. Keep his commands and obey him; serve him and hold fast to him.

DEUTERONOMY 13:4

After the Resurrection, Jesus reminded His disciples of all He had taught them during His three years with them, and at the empty tomb, the angels said: 'Remember how he told you, while he was still with you in Galilee: The Son of Man *must* be delivered into the hands of sinful men, be crucified and on the third day be raised again' (Luke 24:6-7, my italics).

By His Holy Spirit, Christ challenges us with the same 'must'. 'You will be told what you *must* do' (Acts 9:6, my italics), God said to Paul, and a little later, God sent Ananias to Paul saying: 'I will show him how much he *must* suffer for my name' (Acts 9:16, my italics).

Paul and Barnabas taught the same message to their young converts in Galatia: 'We *must* go through many hardships to enter the kingdom of God' (Acts 14:22, my italics).

But when he, the Spirit of truth, comes, he will guide you into all the truth. He will not speak on his own; he will speak only what he hears, and he will tell you what is yet to come.

JOHN 16:13

What we *are* determines what we *do*. Jesus Himself made this abundantly clear in His great Sermon on the Mount. The first section of the Beatitudes show us what we are to be by the grace of God. We are to be poor in spirit rather than proud, mournful for sin rather than indifferent, meek in submission rather than obstinate, hungry and thirsty for God's righteousness rather than for worldly success, merciful and compassionate rather than vindictive and judgmental, pure in heart rather than conformed to a socially acceptable low ethic, peacemakers rather than troublemakers, willing to be persecuted rather than to compromise.

> He said: 'Blessed are the poor in spirit, for theirs is the kingdom of heaven. Blessed are those who mourn, for they will be comforted. Blessed are the meek, for they will inherit the earth. Blessed are those who hunger and thirst for righteousness, for they will be filled. Blessed are the merciful, for they will be shown mercy. Blessed are the pure in heart, for they will see God. Blessed are the peacemakers, for they will be called children of God. Blessed are those who are persecuted because of righteousness, for theirs is the kingdom of heaven.'
>
> MATTHEW 5:3-10

Almighty God, in His terrible, awe-some, holy Majesty, is a 'jealous' God (where jealousy means intolerance of unfaithfulness). He is jealous for my undivided love and loyalty. He is jealous that I should be holy. He has commanded me to have no graven image, no second cause, no ulterior motive, no selfish factor – but that I should love, obey and serve *Him* only.

> *You shall have no other gods before me.*

> *You shall not make for yourself an idol in the form of anything in heaven above or on the earth beneath or in the waters below. You shall not bow down to them or worship them; for I, the L*ORD *your God, am a jealous God … showing love to a thousand generations of those who love me and keep my commandments.* (Exod. 20:3-6)

This jealousy of God is *fire* – fire that can burn out sin and dross, fire that can melt and warm our hard and cold hearts, fire that can purify and harden our will to obey, and fire that can heat and shine through our lives in daily service to others.

In this you greatly rejoice, though now for a little while you may have had to suffer grief in all kinds of trials. These have come so that your faith – of greater worth than gold, which perishes even though refined by fire – may be proved genuine and may result in praise, glory and honour when Jesus Christ is revealed.

1 PETER 1:6-7

LIVING
SACRIFICE

There was no other good enough to pay the price of sin;
He only could unlock the gate of heaven and let us in.

CECIL F. ALEXANDER

The well-known words of childhood hymns became more precious, more meaningful, as one sought to enter into an understanding of the Mystery.

If He so loved me that He was willing to die for me, whatever could I do for Him even to begin to show my heart's longing to thank Him? 'A full, perfect, and sufficient SACRIFICE' – sufficient, sufficient for the sin of the whole world. So no more could be offered. The only possible acceptable SACRIFICE was complete. Christ had SACRIFICED Himself, once for all – once for all time, once for all people, once for all sin. No further SACRIFICE was needed or possible. God had shown Himself satisfied by that perfect offering when He brought back the Lord Jesus Christ from the dead, raising Him to life again that first Easter morning. I could add nothing to the efficacy of His SACRIFICE: I could do nothing to save myself from the penalty of my sins. He had done it all.

And by that will, we have been made
holy through the sacrifice of the body
of Jesus Christ once for all.

HEBREWS 10:10

For twenty years, anything I had needed I had asked of God and He had provided. Now, this night, the Almighty had stooped to ask of *me* something that He condescended to appear to need, and He offered me the *privilege* of responding. He wanted my body, in which to live, and through which to love these very rebel soldiers in the height of their wickedness. It was inconceivable, yet true. He offered me the inestimable privilege of sharing with Him in some little measure, at least, in the edge of the fellowship of His sufferings. And it was all privilege.

For that night, cost became swallowed up in privilege.

Therefore, since Christ suffered in his body, arm yourselves also with the same attitude, because whoever suffers in the body is done with sin.

1 PETER 4:1

To love the Lord my God with all my soul will involve a spiritual cost. I'll have to give Him my heart, and let Him love through it whom and how He wills, even if this seems at times to break my heart.

To love the Lord my God with all my soul will involve a volitional and emotional cost. I'll have to give Him my will, my rights to decide and choose, and all my relationships, for Him to guide and control, even when I cannot understand His reasoning.

So then, those who suffer according to God's will should commit themselves to their faithful Creator and continue to do good.

1 PETER 4:19

To love the Lord my God with all my mind will involve an intellectual cost. I must give Him my mind, my intelligence, my reasoning powers, and trust Him to work through them, even when He may appear to act in contradiction to common sense.

To love the Lord my God with all my strength will involve a physical cost. I must give Him my body to indwell, and through which to speak, whether He chooses by health or sickness, by strength or weakness, and trust Him utterly with the outcome.

And if the Spirit of him who raised Jesus from the dead is living in you, he who raised Christ from the dead will also give life to your mortal bodies because of his Spirit who lives in you.

ROMANS 8:11

The sheer wonder of the greatness of His SACRIFICE for me broke my heart afresh. He so loved *me* that He gave Himself for *me*. He was *my* ransom. He bore *my* sins and iniquities, and with His stripes I was healed. And He was inviting me to identify with Him and with the Africans among whom He had placed me as His witness. If I were willing to let Him whittle away the protective bark – this ability to withdraw or to become impersonal so as not to be hurt by, or finally involved in, a situation – He would bring me into a new oneness with Himself and with others.

> *He himself bore our sins in his body on the tree, so that we might die to sins and live for righteousness; by his wounds you have been healed.*
>
> 1 PETER 2:24

The first major 'cost' that I encountered in seeking to love God with all my heart was in the giving up of my pride – pride of nationality, pride of education, pride of natural abilities. God has continually to break me on each of these. They get in the way of love, real outgoing love. Then He has to deal with my self – self-reliance, self-justification, self-pity. These too hinder the free flow of His love. Step by step, as God deals with pride and the insidious love of self, He can take my heart and truly love others through it.

To love God with all my heart is to give Him my heart, that He may fill it and overflow it with His own self-giving love for all among whom He sends me to live.

> But your hearts must be fully committed to the LORD our God, to live by his decrees and obey his commands, as at this time.
>
> 1 KINGS 8:61

God has a perfect plan for each one of us, a plan that fits into His overall purpose for the whole world. My individual liberty is safeguarded within His plan, insofar as I am free to choose to accept or reject it: but once I have accepted it, I must give obedience to Him within it, and learn to say wholeheartedly: 'Not my will, but thine be done.' If I truly believe in Him, I'll trust Him to desire for me that which is for my highest good, and to have planned for its fulfilment.

'For I know the plans I have for you,' declares the Lord, 'plans to prosper you and not to harm you, plans to give you hope and a future'.

JEREMIAH 29:11

I long to be kept by God in an attitude of willing surrender so that He can go on to perfect that which concerns me; so that He can go on stripping and whittling and sandpapering until He is content with the new arrow He is creating.

Crucifixion, the death-to-self life, must surely be seen by us all as costly, but the abundant life that He wishes to bestow on each can only be seen as unutterable privilege.

For momentary, light affliction is producing for us an eternal weight of glory far beyond all comparison. (2 Cor. 4:17, NASB)

For if, by the trespass of the one man, death reigned through that one man, how much more will those who receive God's abundant provision of grace and of the gift of righteousness reign in life through the one man, Jesus Christ!

ROMANS 5:17

He died once for all – for all sins, for all men, for all time. He cried: *'It is finished!'* (John 19:30). There can be no further SACRIFICE for sin.

Then what is my part? How can I respond? What SACRIFICE can I make to Him and for Him, to show the depth of my love in response to all He has done for me?

The psalmist declares that he will offer to God *'a SACRIFICE of thanksgiving'* as he calls on His name (Ps. 116:17). The writer to the Hebrews exhorts them to offer up continually *'a SACRIFICE of praise'* to God as they acknowledge His name (Heb. 13:15). He stresses that doing good and sharing what we have with others less well provided for are *'SACRIFICES ... well-pleasing to God'* (Heb. 13:16, AMP).

The sacrifices of God are a broken spirit; a broken and contrite heart, O God, you will not despise.

PSALM 51:17

Paul, a doctor of law and philosophy, a respected member of the Sanhedrin, a revered leader of the people, 'had it made', as we would say today. He would never need to think about how to pay the mortgage or educate his children, or provide for the family in his old age. He need never fear dismissal from a job or unemployment. Then he met with the Lord Jesus Christ. His life was revolutionized. He suddenly had a new goal, a new purpose, a new zeal and fervour. *'But whatever things were gain to me,'* he said, *'those things I have counted as loss for the sake of Christ. More than that, I count all things to be loss in view of the surpassing value of knowing Christ Jesus my Lord, for whom I have suffered the loss of all things, and count them but rubbish in order that I may gain Christ'* (Phil. 3:7-8, NASB). Paul gave up *all* in order to follow Christ, and to take the Good News to Asia Minor and Greece and Italy. *'SACRIFICES ... well-pleasing to God.'*

> *Be imitators of God, therefore, as dearly loved children and live a life of love, just as Christ loved us and gave himself up for us as a fragrant offering and sacrifice to God.*
>
> EPHESIANS 5:1-2

The early Christians in the first and second centuries hazarded their lives for love of Christ. They were a despised, illegal group, and knew that at any moment imperial Rome might attempt to crush them out of existence: yet they refused to compromise, or worship Caesar, or offer pagan SACRIFICES. They continued to meet for worship even when hounded from pillar to post. They sang praises to the Lord, even when they were being burned at the stake, or being torn limb from limb in the arena. They refused to be stamped out. Through each succeeding wave of bitter persecution, their faith and courage grew, and they offered 'SACRIFICES... well-pleasing to God.'

Blessed are you when people insult you, persecute you and falsely say all kinds of evil against you because of me. Rejoice and be glad, because great is your reward in heaven, for in the same way they persecuted the prophets who were before you.

MATTHEW 5:11-12

Today it would appear that we Christians prefer to talk of a measure of commitment, the length to which we are willing to become involved, rather than the depths of God's immeasurable love in which we long to become immersed. There is abroad an atmosphere of careful calculation, 'thus far and no further', maintaining certain reasonable limits. The carefree abandonment of love that marks the *SACRIFICES* of Paul, of second-century Christians, of nineteenth-century missionaries, seems sadly lacking. Today we weigh up what we can afford to give Him: in those days, they knew that they could not afford to give Him less than all!

Take delight in the LORD, and he will give you the desires of your heart.

Commit your way to the LORD; trust in him and he will do this: He will make your righteous reward shine like the dawn, your vindication like the noonday sun.

PSALM 37:5-6

The Lord is pleading with us for full surrender, an absolute, willing SACRIFICE of all I consider mine, which certainly will include my rights to decide and choose and act on my own initiative. It is not enough to give mental assent to doctrinal teaching. There must be a practical, realistic response. The plea is for action. 'Present your bodies [all that you are] as a living … SACRIFICE' (Rom. 12:1, ESV). The Christian is invited to give God all, to make Him indisputably King over every part of life: to become, as it were, His bondslave in total obedience to His will.

I am the LORD your God, consecrate yourselves and be holy, because I am holy.

LEVITICUS 11:44

To be a living SACRIFICE will involve all my love. My emotions and desires are to be actively dedicated to the Lord, with one burning desire, to worship Him more worthily and to serve Him more wholeheartedly. I relinquish the right to choose whom I will love and how, giving the Lord the right to choose for me. This is not fatalism, but a responsible act of my free will, and I must consciously seek to know His will and direction. I accept His law in His Word as my standard in this, as in all other departments of my life. Whether I have a life partner or not is wholly His to decide, and I accept gladly His best will for my life. I must bring all the areas of my affections to the Lord for His control, for here, above all else, I need to SACRIFICE my right to choose for myself. I dare not trust myself in this area. God knows that which is in my own best interest, and which will make me more wholly available to Himself for the fulfilling of His perfect law of liberty.

Consecrate yourselves and be holy, because I am the Lord your God.

LEVITICUS 20:7

As I began to live the life of faith I slowly began to see and understand that everything in life relates to God. This living faith which creates a vital relationship between the Creator and each of His creatures is a free gift of God, available to all and to any who will accept it. This living faith is the most tremendous fact of the Christian way of life. It is, in itself, independent of feelings (though our appreciation of it frequently involves an emotional response). It cannot be earned or merited. It must be accepted as a gift, and then practised as a way of life. I have had to learn continuously to 'live by faith', rather than by feelings.

This vital relationship to God has to be constantly asserted as a fact, resting on the historic events of Calvary and the empty tomb and independent of whether I happen to feel saved, or at peace, or in touch with God, or whether I happen to be discouraged, filled with doubts, or sensing personal unworthiness.

I, the LORD, refuse to accept anyone who is proud. Only those who live by faith are acceptable to me.

HABAKKUK 2:4, CEV

LIVING
FAITH

In the early days of our spiritual lives, there is often much to encourage and inspire our FAITH. This was certainly true for me personally – remarkable answers to prayer (too detailed and too numerous to be shrugged off as coincidences) and financial deliverances in times of need (sometimes accurate to the last penny and designated exactly, with no foreknowledge on the part of the donors). Initially we may think that our FAITH is increased by these miracles of God's giving. We feel this is so. Actually our FAITH, which is God's gift to us, cannot be increased; it is our realization of the *fact* of our relationship to God that grows.

Later, God may withhold some of the more startling, or more miraculous, manifestations of His giving, in order to establish us in the realization of our FAITH, independently of its fruit. At this time, our appreciation of the spirit of giving as the fruit of FAITH will gradually change from the childlike joy of receiving that which is given, to the adult joy of giving that which others may receive. Our FAITH, now firmly established, will be demonstrated in a spirit of self-giving that would have been inconceivable to us before the Spirit of God took over our lives.

We have different gifts, according to the grace given to each of us. If a man's gift is prophesying, let him use it in proportion to his faith. If it is serving, let him serve; if it is teaching, let him teach; if it is encouraging, let him encourage; if it is contributing to the needs of others, let him give generously.

ROMANS 12:6-8

God's plan is already complete. Each of us is created to fit into that plan:

For we are his workmanship, created in Christ Jesus for good works, which God prepared beforehand, that we should walk in them (Eph. 2:10, ESV).

When we ask God to guide us, we are asking to be shown the job He has already 'prepared in advance for us to do'. We are simply stating a willingness now to go His way for us, instead of continuing in our own way (Isa. 53:6). It is by the FAITH of the Son of God indwelling me that I am assured that God has a place for me. It is by this same FAITH that I grow to realize that outside of God's prepared place, there is no ultimate satisfaction or peace of heart for me, and so I desire to be led into His will for my life.

*He guides me along the right paths
for his name's sake.*

PSALM 23:3

So God cares for us as we travel the road mapped out by Him, for our life's journey. The rules are plain for us to follow in obedience. As we obey each step of the way, so will the problems be resolved, and the next stretch become clear to us. The directions God gives us, that we may know Him and read His map for us, do not include a blueprint for omniscience, that we may know what is around the next corner before we reach it, but rather a blueprint for intelligent obedience that will enable us to reach and turn the next corner safely, whatever we meet around it. We are not advised to ask God *why* the road curves, but to ask God's wisdom to follow the curves carefully and without accident. When we meet a parked car, it is not of interest to us to know *why* it is parked there, but it is of paramount importance to us to know the rules as to how to pass it, that we may not put ourselves or other road users in unnecessary danger, by passing on the wrong side.

He guides the humble in what is right
and teaches them his way.

PSALM 25:9

So what is God's highway code? Where are all these directions to be found? Surely in His written Word, the Bible. I pray that God may stir up my FAITH in His Word as *the* compelling force to direct and control my life. His standards are clearly set forth, and His commands with regard to keeping those standards are equally explicit. The more frequently, the more regularly, and the more prayerfully that I read the Bible, the more sure I shall be of the path that He has planned for me. God teaches me clearly through the example of the life of His Son, our Lord Jesus Christ, recorded in the gospels. By His life and His teaching, Christ reveals to us the character of God. Paul, Peter and John in their epistles, under the inspiration of the Holy Spirit, take this teaching and apply it to our lives, that thereby we may become like Him – *'conformed to the image of his Son'* (Rom. 8:29). The Old Testament abounds with signposts to help us – examples to follow, warnings to heed, failures to shun, precepts to obey.

Set up road signs; put up guideposts. Take note of the highway, the road that you take.

JEREMIAH 31:21

This last point is probably the cornerstone. If as we read and study the Word, we seek grace to obey God's revealed precepts, we shall find guidance; that is, we *shall* discover that we are being guided day by day, possibly often without actually realizing it. So often when I am fumbling about, seeking guidance, feeling that all is dark, and unable to see any familiar landmarks, not even the glimmer of a 'cat's eye', the reason for my fog is disobedience to a clearly stated precept. For example, it is unrealistic to seek special guidance as to whether I should or should not do a certain action, when the action concerned is sinful according to scriptural standards. I do not have to seek guidance as to whether or not I should marry an unbeliever or date a married man, any more than whether or not I should falsify my income tax returns or lie to a customs officer. In each of these cases I need to ask for a spirit of obedience to God's commands, rather than for guidance as to my reactions. If indulged in, these would each be acts of disobedience. Not only do they not in themselves, therefore, pose a problem of guidance, but they may, if persisted in, even cause an absence of guidance. A realization of guidance is dependent on concurrent obedience to God's revealed will.

This is what the Lord says: 'Stand at the crossroads
and look; ask for the ancient paths,
ask where the good way is, and walk in it, and
you will find rest for your souls.'

JEREMIAH 6:16

God's leadership is always conscious, and He never sets a pace that we cannot maintain. When the corners come, He is there waiting for us, to take us around safely. We must just stay close enough to see the guiding light continuously, or hear accurately the directions of the still small voice. Guidance is a very personal business. Basic rules are there for us all; the code book is to be studied by every traveller. However, the actual route and pace are decided separately for each individual. Following the one who has gone before (as it were, the car ahead) is fine if we know that it is heading for the same destination as we are, and if we are sure that the driver himself knows the way.

With God, we know that He knows the way we should take, and that He will make no mistake in guiding us to our true destination, but how can we be sure that we are following Him, obeying His direction, listening to His voice?

I will lead the blind by ways they have not known, along unfamiliar paths I will guide them; I will turn the darkness into light before them and make the rough places smooth. These are the things I will do; I will not forsake them.

ISAIAH 42:16

Each one of us needs to be stirred in our FAITH, to go wherever God would send us. This may be far or near. Usually it will simply be a moving forward in the obvious line of duty, with no 'extra' word of guidance. God has promised to check us if we deviate from the way but not necessarily to applaud us if we remain constantly in the way.

> *And your ears will hear a word behind you, 'This is the way, walk in it', whenever you turn to the right or to the left* (Isa. 30:21, NASB).

**You have made known to me the paths of life;
you will fill me with joy in your presence.**

ACTS 2:28

Over and over again, we come back to His omnipotent sovereignty and perfect predetermined counsel of omniscient will. He cannot and will not make mistakes. Our FAITH is in Him, not in the outworking that we see among our frail selves in our fallen human nature. Our FAITH in God is unassailable and unshakeable. He does know the end from the beginning, and He can move me into or out of circumstances in the working out of His total purpose just as He wishes. I am wholly God's, and as I am His servant, He has no need to explain to me the why and the wherefore of His dealings and His methods. God asks of me one step at a time in obedience and in FAITH. He may only show me one yard ahead at a time; that is enough to establish my FAITH so that He can equally show me all the other yards ahead in the years to come.

To this you were called, because Christ suffered for you, leaving you an example, that you should follow in his steps.

1 PETER 2:21

God's guidance includes the circumstances in which we find ourselves, the advice of older Christian friends, examples seen in our daily reading in the Bible, the assurance that develops in our hearts as we pray over a situation, and an increasing consciousness of peace as all these fit together and add up to one solution.

At different times in our lives, one of these means of guidance may be more prominent than another. All have had their part in my own life. Sometimes God does graciously allow us to use fleeces, though it would seem to be the least reliable means of guidance, lending itself to abuse, and possibly stemming from a lack of trust or a desire for haste.

Since we live by the Spirit,
let us keep in step with the Spirit.

GALATIANS 5:25

Whether my prayer can affect a situation or not may cease to be a relevant question if I can understand the purpose of prayer. If I believe that prayer is the natural outcome of my relationship with God by which I learn to know and understand His will and purpose, and so seek to bring my life into line for its fulfilment, I shall not *primarily* be seeking to 'affect situations'.

Any understanding of the point or power of prayer demands a real exercise of FAITH.

Without FAITH in God, we shall not seek to obey His command to 'pray without ceasing'. We must believe that God is, that He cares and that He can answer.

Trust in the LORD with all your heart and lean not on your own understanding; in all your ways submit to him, and he will make your paths straight.

PROVERBS 3:5-6

God has commanded me to pray. Christ lived in a spirit of prayer and taught us to pray in like manner. As we read the gospel story, we can see just how dependent Christ was on prayer to maintain His relationship with His Father. In praying, He found courage to vanquish Satan during the temptations in the wilderness. Through prayer, the realization of the authority of God enabled Christ to cure the sick, heal the leper, and cast out demons throughout His ministry (Luke 4:42). Prayer channelled to Him the wisdom of God that enabled Him to reason with the doctors of the law and refute the subtleties of the scribes (Luke 5:16). Through prayer, Christ was guided to choose and appoint the twelve apostles, even knowing that Judas would later betray Him (Luke 6:12). It was through Christ's prayer that Peter was given the great revelation as to who Christ was: *'Thou art the Christ, the Son of the living God'* (Matt 16:16, KJV). As a result of His prayer life, our Lord was able to teach His disciples about the suffering of the Cross that lay ahead of Him. *'As he was praying'* He was transfigured in glory before the amazed eyes of His three special friends (Luke 9:29). When He descended to the sin-torn world in the valley, it was through prayer that He healed the epileptic boy (Matt. 17:17). In prayer Christ found strength to set His face to go to Jerusalem (Luke 9:51). He taught His disciples through His own prayer life the secret of receiving from the Father all that was needed for their ministry (Luke 11:1-13).

But when you pray, go into your room, close the door and pray to your Father, who is unseen. Then your Father, who sees what is done in secret, will reward you.

MATTHEW 6:6

Christ showed us the courage and fearlessness that we can receive in the face of persecution and opposition. He showed us His deep concern for the salvation of men as He wept over Jerusalem (Luke 13:34) and for all mankind (Luke 22:44). He exhorted us through parables (Luke 18:1, 9) and miracles (Luke 18:38), directly (Luke 21:36 and 22:39-46) and indirectly (Luke 21:37) to *pray* – for ourselves, for each other, for the world.

Yes, prayer is obviously a vital factor in putting God's plan into practice. Not only must I recognize this, I must also believe in the *need* to put God's plan into practice, if I am to take part in prayer effectively.

> *Therefore I tell you, whatever you ask*
> *for in prayer, believe that you have*
> *received it, and it will be yours.*
>
> MARK 11:24

If we would ask God to give us a like concern for the vast multitudes in the world who are yet without any knowledge of Christ; if we would honestly seek to be identified with the needs of those who are crushed by the cruel despotism of Satan and his evil hosts, held in blindness and ignorance of God's grace and love; if we would allow our hearts to be filled with Christ's compassion for the spiritually blind and hungry, we too would be enabled by God to look ahead to our reward. Christ endured the Cross for 'the joy set before Him'. He could see by FAITH the fruit of His obedience unto death, that is to say, the salvation of countless millions through the ages, and be satisfied. We too can believe that by accepting God's burden and thereby being driven to pray, we shall see the results in lives set free from Satan's clutches. This will indeed be reward enough for all of us.

If you have any encouragement from being united with Christ, if any comfort from his love, if any fellowship with the Spirit, if any tenderness and compassion, then make my joy complete by being like-minded, having the same love, being one in spirit and purpose. Do nothing out of selfish ambition or vain conceit, but in humility consider others better than yourselves.

PHILIPPIANS 2:1-3

To care deeply for lost multitudes throughout the world, and thus to be burdened to pray for their salvation is only possible as we have FAITH in God and FAITH in the fact that He is able and willing to answer our prayers. We do not need to know why God is so willing to act in response to our prayers nor how He does it. The reasons and mechanisms are known only to our omniscient and omnipotent God. We know that He has chosen that it should be so. He wants His adopted children to see the needs of others, to be concerned on their behalf, and to show their trust in Him as their Father by bringing that concern to Him in prayer. God has commanded that we should pray at all times – importunate, fervent prayers – believing, persistent prayers.

> *The harvest is plentiful, but the workers are few. Therefore beseech the Lord of the harvest to send out workers into His harvest* (Matt. 9:37-38, NASB) [is Christ's command to us].

I urge, then, first of all, that petitions, prayers, intercession and thanksgiving be made for all people.

1 TIMOTHY 2:1

God always hears and answers prayer but not necessarily just as we anticipate. As we pray in FAITH, in the power of His name, seeking to know His will and in obedience to His commands, He answers – according to His perfect will as is best for each one concerned. It is not a matter of *yes* or *no* or even *wait*. As we draw apart into a consciousness of His presence, making ourselves available to the Holy Spirit to pray through us, God is willing to enable us to see things from His viewpoint (even if, as yet, but dimly). We find ourselves burdened to pray for different individuals or situations, as God puts the burden upon our hearts. It rejoices the heart of the Father that we are becoming willing to share the burden that rests on His own heart, and that we desire to be filled with His compassion for the hungry multitude around us. We may not as yet fully comprehend His will in all the fullness of His purposes, but as bit by bit we are enabled to understand something of His burden and to pray accordingly, wanting only His will and to be pleasing to Him, then He graciously answers our prayers beyond all we can ask or think. In this way we can come to know more clearly what God's will really is in a situation, as we watch His answers to our prayers, for these very answers reveal to us His actual will and purpose in that particular situation.

Therefore confess your sins to each other and pray for each other so that you may be healed. The prayer of a righteous person is powerful and effective.

JAMES 5:16

How do we know if we are praying 'according to His will'? He sees the motives of our hearts. If I sincerely want His will, even though my prayer may be wrongly worded or my expectation of His answer may be wrongly directed, He *will* answer 'according to his will'. Thus by watching the answers to my prayers, I can learn to understand more clearly and accurately what is His will. Thus gradually my praying will become more in line with His will, as He enables me to think His thoughts and see His plan. Granted that my heart motive in prayer is honestly 'not my will but yours be done', when an answer to prayer is not what I expected it to be, that will show me, that in that instance, I had not properly understood His will. His answers to sincere praying reveal to us His will.

To learn to wait expectantly *will become the attitude of my heart in the practice of prayer, that I may thereby discover His perfect will in each situation.*

This is the confidence we have in approaching God: that if we ask anything according to his will, he hears us.

1 JOHN 5:14

FAITH is exciting to a Christian. It is a blank cheque duly signed by God, giving the drawer access to the unlimited riches of heavenly grace. We can take 'by FAITH' all that God has prepared for us in His abundant, outpoured generosity, as we endorse the 'cheque by prayer and FAITH, presenting it to our heavenly Father in accordance with His will.

> *Things which eye has not seen and ear has not heard, and – which have not entered the heart of man. All that God has prepared for those who love Him. For to us God revealed them through the Spirit.* (1 Cor. 2:9-10, NASB)

To the worldly-wise person, following human reasoning and banking on his meagre experience through his five senses, all this may seem utterly foolish or even presumptuous. It is impossible without FAITH to understand the ways of FAITH. The man of FAITH must not be surprised or depressed that he cannot help the worldly man to comprehend these ways of God. It is just not possible.

And without faith it is impossible to please God, because anyone who comes to him must believe that he exists and that he rewards those who earnestly seek him.

HEBREWS 11:6

All Christians, not just a select few, are made new creatures in Christ Jesus and thereafter called to become His ambassadors, entrusted with the word of reconciliation – sent out to represent our Lord and to teach His message throughout the world. Christ's last command to us, before He ascended back into heaven, was that we should be His witnesses *'in Jerusalem, and in all Judea and Samaria, and even to the remotest part of the earth'* (Acts 1:8, NASB).

God gives His gift of *FAITH* to *be* Christian witnesses, His ambassadors – not just to give, to go, to pray, but to be. We are to be available to God all the time, so that we can act in obedience (giving what He commands us); so that we can challenge the powers of darkness (going where He sends us); and so that we can keep on believing in the midst of every type of discouragement (praying as He burdens us). In all of this, our FAITH will be tried, as gold by fire – purifying, refining, enriching it – as we translate FAITH into service for Him.

We are therefore Christ's ambassadors, as though God were making his appeal through us.

2 CORINTHIANS 5:20

LIVING
FELLOWSHIP

The Cross has to be the common attraction that draws members into the closely knit FELLOWSHIP of the local church. However, this *koinonia* is not an exclusive club; it is not divisive and it is certainly not man-orientated. It is inclusive of all who believe; it is unitive for all who place their trust in Christ as Lord and Saviour; it is self-abnegating, as each member seeks to give for the good of others in the FELLOWSHIP rather than to get from the group for one's own benefit. It is a FELLOWSHIP based on love and loyalty, understanding and trust; a desire to see the other person's point of view rather than to gain one's own way; a willingness to be ignored, overlooked or misunderstood if this should be for the general good.

God is faithful, who has called you into fellowship with his Son, Jesus Christ our Lord.

1 CORINTHIANS 1:9

The doctrinal meaning of *koinonia*, as it is promised to all members of the visible Church of the Lord Jesus Christ here on earth, can only be rightly understood as we recognise the FELLOWSHIP that exists between the three Persons of the Trinity.

These three Persons act together, most noticeably in creation and in the redemption of mankind, in perfect harmony. We can hear God saying in Genesis 1:26: 'Let us make man in our image', and then read of each Person of the Trinity playing His part in that creative act:

> *In the beginning God created the heavens and the earth… and the Spirit of God was hovering over the waters* (Gen. 1:1-2).

> *God… has spoken to us by his Son… through whom he made the universe* (Heb. 1:2).

> *In the beginning was the Word… and the Word was God… Through him all things were made* (John 1:1-3).

They work in the same harmony in procuring the redemption of man.

> *May the grace of the Lord Jesus Christ, and the love of God, and the fellowship of the Holy Spirit be with you all.*
>
> 2 CORINTHIANS 13:14

God the Father preordained that His Son should be put to death 'by nailing him to the cross' (Acts 2:23) and so He chose us in Christ 'before the creation of the world' (Eph. 1:4).

God the Son 'loved [us] ... and gave himself for [us]' (Gal. 2:20). Did He not say, of the Good Shepherd, 'I lay down my life… No one takes it from me, but I lay it down of my own accord' (John 10:17-18)?

God the Spirit makes this redemption real in the heart of each believer. Not only are we to be 'born of the Spirit' (John 3:8) and so become 'new creation[s]' in Christ (2 Cor. 5:17), but we are to know that we are saved; we are to understand what God has wrought for us. 'God has revealed [all this] ... to us by his Spirit' (1 Cor. 2:10).

This harmonious working of the Trinity brings peace into the heart of each believer. '[T]he Counsellor, the Holy Spirit, whom the Father will send in my name,' Christ said to His disciples, 'will teach you all things and will remind you of everything I have said to you. Peace I leave with you,' Christ continued, as though the very presence of the Holy Spirit would in itself bestow that very peace. 'My peace I give you' (John 14:26-7).

'Christ Jesus… is our peace,' Paul wrote to the Ephesians, as he explained how, by His death on the Cross, Christ had broken down the dividing wall of hostility that existed between us and God, and between us and others: 'His purpose was to create in himself one new man out of the two, thus making peace' (Eph. 2:13-15).

> *We proclaim to you what we have seen and heard, so that you also may have fellowship with us. And our fellowship is with the Father and with his Son, Jesus Christ.*
>
> 1 JOHN 1:3-4

Furthermore, the three Persons of the Trinity not only work together in perfect FELLOWSHIP, but also they claim equality, the One with each Other. The Son, our Lord Jesus Christ, claimed equality and unity with His Father, and the Father and the Son state they are equal to the Spirit: 'I and the Father are one,' Jesus explicitly stated (John 10:30).

> 'My Father is always at his work to this very day, and I, too, am working.' For this reason the Jews tried all the harder to kill him; not only was he breaking the Sabbath, but he was even calling God his own Father, making himself equal with God (John 5:17-18).

> Your attitude should be the same as that of Christ Jesus: Who, being in very nature God, did not consider equality with God something to be grasped.
>
> PHILIPPIANS 2:5-6

Jesus prayed that Christians would know this same unity among themselves as He and His Father and the Spirit enjoyed among themselves (John 17:21-3): '...that all of them may be one, Father, just as you are in me and I am in you. May they also be in us so that the world may believe that you have sent me. I have given them the glory that you gave me, that they may be one as we are one: I in them and you in me. May they be brought to complete unity...'

Such unity will indeed be the basis of true FELLOWSHIP, and this in turn will bring about true peace.

> *Make every effort to keep the unity of*
> *the Spirit through the bond of peace.*
>
> EPHESIANS 4:3

For not only are we to enter into true FELLOWSHIP with God, but this is also then to work out into FELLOWSHIP with other members of the Body. John declares that we are to 'have FELLOWSHIP with one another' (1 John 1:7-10). Here again, this FELLOWSHIP has to flow out of a clearly understood relationship which will manifest itself in practical ways to the common good. Luke described this so clearly between believers in the early Church:

> *Those who accepted [Peter's] message were baptised, and about three thousand were added to [the Church's] number that day. They devoted themselves to the apostles' teaching and to the FELLOWSHIP, to the breaking of bread and to prayer. Everyone was filled with awe, and many wonders and miraculous signs were done by the apostles. All the believers were together and had everything in common. Selling their possessions and goods, they gave to anyone as he had need. Every day they continued to meet together in the temple courts. They broke bread in their homes and ate together with glad and sincere hearts, praising God and enjoying the favour of all the people.* (Acts 2:41-7)

The life appeared; we have seen it and testify to it, and we proclaim to you the eternal life, which was with the Father and has appeared to us. We proclaim to you what we have seen and heard, so that you also may have fellowship with us. And our fellowship is with the Father and with his Son, Jesus Christ. We write this to make our joy complete.

1 JOHN 1:2-3

True FELLOWSHIP is actually right relationships worked out in our lives in practical ways. Such relationships bring peace. This is the peace that He made available to us when He died on the Cross as our substitute; it is 'the peace of God that transcends all understanding' (Phil. 4:7).

Peace is the obvious and invariable fruit of biblical *koinonia* – FELLOWSHIP with God, FELLOWSHIP with our fellow-men, and FELLOWSHIP in suffering 'for his name' – peace with God, peace with ourselves, and peace with each other.

Let the peace of Christ rule in your hearts, since as members of one body you were called to peace. And be thankful.

COLOSSIANS 3:15

How succinct is the writing of the Holy Spirit!

Complete in Him (Col. 2:10, KJV).

In three short words He sums up the basis of all true FELLOWSHIP – that is, the relationship of being united to Him.

And Who is the 'him'? None other than God Almighty, revealed to us in all His fullness by the Lord Jesus Christ, the Word made flesh and dwelling among us. Paul wrote, 'For in him [Christ] dwelleth all the fullness of the Godhead bodily. And ye are complete in him…' (Col. 2:9-10, KJV).

And if we are 'complete in him', it does not take a vast training in logic to deduce that we are *in*complete *out of* Him.

Therefore if you have any encouragement from being united with Christ, if any comfort from his love, if any common sharing in the Spirit, if any tenderness and compassion, then make my joy complete by being like-minded, having the same love, being one in spirit and of one mind.

PHILIPPIANS 2:1-2

Yes, there is a great God, who created all the wonderful and beautiful world around us, and also men and women in that world, that we might love, serve and worship Him. But over the years we men have chosen to love, serve and worship ourselves, rather than God. And what a mess we have made of God's world as a result. The great God has written a book (holding my Bible in my hand) in which He calls that mess *sin*. And He, the Creator, has judged that the wages of sin, our just deserts that each one of us has earned by our own free choice, is death, that is to say, spiritual death – to live eternally separated from Him who would have been our friend and counsellor.

For the wages of sin is death, but the gift of God is eternal life in Christ Jesus our Lord.

ROMANS 6: 23

No prayer can give God greater delight or be more certainly 'according to his will' and therefore to be prayed 'in his name', than that short one: 'Please, God, cross out my "I", so that others see and hear Jesus in and through me, instead of myself.' If my sole desire is that my relationship to my Lord and Saviour should be close, real and vital at all times, God will undoubtedly overrule every other outward circumstance that seeks to attack my peace of mind and to break my relationship with God. He will see to the smooth running of that which He Himself has created, to achieve His perfect purpose.

> *Therefore, my dear friends, as you have always obeyed – not only in my presence, but now much more in my absence – continue to work out your salvation with fear and trembling, for it is God who works in you to will and to act in order to fulfill his good purpose.*
>
> PHILIPPIANS 2:12-13

When the divine Son of God was born into this world, He lived a life of unquestioning obedience to His Father. He sought always to do His Father's will, to think His thoughts, speak His words, perform the actions of His purposes; as He Himself said, seeking 'always to please Him'. In the Garden of Gethsemane, falling on His face before His heavenly Father, Christ Jesus prayed with strong tears, 'My Father, if it is possible, may this cup be taken from me. Yet not as I will, but as you will' (Matt. 26:36-9).

> *[Christ Jesus] being in very nature God,*
> *did not consider equality with God*
> *something to be grasped,*
> *but made himself nothing,*
> *taking the very nature of a servant,*
> *being made in human likeness.*
> *And being found in appearance as a man,*
> *he humbled himself*
> *and became obedient to death – even*
> *death on a cross!* (Phil. 2:6-8)

Obey me, and I will be your God and you will be my people. Walk in obedience to all I command you, that it may go well with you.

JEREMIAH 7:23

Our Lord Jesus Christ gave willing, submissive obedience to His Father throughout His whole earthly life, never once rebelling or seeking His own way or choosing an easier path for Himself than that chosen for Him by His Father, even when this included the cruel death by crucifixion. In doing this, He fulfilled all the obedience that we humans have failed to give to God.

Once we reject the servant-role for which God created us and seek to order our own lives, things go wrong. We cannot support the master-role because we were not created for it. When we became sons and daughters of God, this new relationship should have caused us to revert instantaneously to our rightful servant-status in submission to the will of our heavenly Father.

I will be a Father to you, and you will be my sons and daughters, says the Lord Almighty.

2 CORINTHIANS 6:18

To submit is to place ourselves voluntarily under the authority of another; to a Christian, that is specifically to place oneself under the authority of God and His written Word. This is very different from being subjected to the will of another. That is when someone forcibly and determinedly places himself over another, and compels them to obey his will whether they want to or not. God never subjects us to His will, but always seeks that we should submit ourselves to Him, as trusting children to a loving Father.

Submit yourselves, then, to God.
Resist the devil, and he will flee from you.

JAMES 4:7

Am I willing to be under God's authority, seeking to obey in every particular His written Word and to please Him in every part of my life? Do I will to give unquestioning obedience to God? I talk about loving God; I may sing about loving God; but in reality, do I actually love Him to the extent that I am prepared to obey Him – even if I don't always understand why He has made certain laws and imposed certain apparent restrictions? Am I so convinced of His unlimited love for me that I know that any such restriction must be for my good, and should therefore be embraced wholeheartedly? 'Whoever has my commands and obeys them, he is the one who loves me' (John 14:21).

*Jesus replied: 'Love the Lord your God
with all your heart and with all your soul
and with all your mind.'*

MATTHEW 22:37

To enjoy the deep FELLOWSHIP to which we now have access, as children of God, demands that we develop a sense of the Presence of the Eternal as the most important and vivid fact in our daily lives. Every occurrence, every act, every word, must be seen to be part of God's plan for our individual lives. It must become a habit, consciously or subconsciously, to relate every event, big or little, to God, realising it to be part of His plan and purpose. It must become instinctive to ask Him for understanding whenever a doubt or question arises in our minds.

That is what 'being yoked to Christ' means in practical everyday language. I must not allow the devil to separate my living and thinking from my realisation of belonging to God. My whole being is to be linked to Him in a very tangible and inescapable way. I am to be bound to Him by His yoke, I must pull with Him, or else expect to be bruised.

*Take my yoke upon you and learn from me,
for I am gentle and humble in heart, and you
will find rest for your souls. For my yoke is
easy and my burden is light.*

MATTHEW 11:29-30

Have we captured the wonder and splendour of the majesty of our God with the imagination of an artist? Is our sense of awe in the presence of our divine Lover growing keener and deeper? In our prayer life, have we reached that stage when we only seek God, in and for Himself, and not for any of His benefits? Sometimes as we bow before Him in total inner silence, with a deep desire to worship Him and to hear His still small voice, there may come over us an almost shattering conviction of the very presence of God Himself. No longer will we even seek to worship Him, let alone to bother Him with our small and insignificant problems, or to ask His help for success in our little bit of ministry – God fills our horizon.

You make known to me the path of life;
you will fill me with joy in your presence,
with eternal pleasures at your right hand.

PSALM 16:11

We cannot afford to ignore or to forget this; it is the very essence of being alive, of being conscious of life within us. The whole meaning of Christianity is that we live our lives in the presence of Almighty God – that is to say, in FELLOWSHIP with Him. Have we, each one of us, apprehended this truth? Do we live constantly in the presence of the spaceless and unchanging God, the God who not only blazes on our spiritual horizons, but who also lives intimately within the world of present-tense commonplace events?

May he strengthen your hearts so that you will be blameless and holy in the presence of our God and Father when our Lord Jesus comes with all his holy ones.

1 THESSALONIANS 3:13

Equally, our prayer life must become utterly theocentric, centred on God in all His beauty and majesty and power, and in no way dependent on our own subjective feelings and varying needs, nor even on the feelings and needs of those whom we seek to serve. 'Is my God big enough?' someone has asked, or have I tried to contract Him down to a size I can comprehend and 'manage'? God should fill my horizons! He should be vaster than all my comprehension, yet wholly filling all my understanding. Do I perpetually turn to Him, losing myself and my petty interests in His vast unfathomable love and greatness, and refusing to allow even the most pressing work or practical problems to distract me from Him? That is FELLOWSHIP with the Almighty, and only thus will I keep alive the awed sense of the mysteries that I long to share with others.

And let us run with perseverance the race marked out for us, fixing our eyes on Jesus, the pioneer and perfecter of faith. For the joy set before him he endured the cross, scorning its shame, and sat down at the right hand of the throne of God.

HEBREWS 12:1-2

Our inner life must be an ever-deepening awareness of this great and wonderful God. The sense of the presence of God, immeasurably beyond us, will keep us in a constant attitude of humble awe. Yet He is so closely with us that we can cling to Him in trust and loyal love.

This transcendent God is the One who invites us to be yoked to Him!

This God became our Saviour. He, the Almighty, the Majestic, the Creator:

> …*made himself nothing,*
> *taking the very nature of a servant,*
> *being made in human likeness…*
> *he humbled himself*
> *and became obedient to death – even death on a cross!*
> (Phil. 2:6-8)

> *Who among the gods is like you, LORD?*
> *Who is like you – majestic in holiness,*
> *awesome in glory, working wonders?*
>
> EXODUS 15:11

In that profoundly simple sermon, the Master-Preacher taught us that we were to be perfect as the Father was perfect (Matt. 5:48). How can we be perfect as He was? In Matthew 5:38-48 He reveals Himself to us as being perfect in meekness, commanding us not to resist evil; He was perfect in generosity, commanding us to give to the one who asks us; He was perfect in compassion, commanding us to love our enemies and pray for those who persecute us. Humanly speaking, all this is beyond us, beyond our wildest dreams, totally impossible, too other-worldly, we think, ever to work in this hurly-burly world in which we live. And yet, as we walk in step with Him, He will show us that it is possible, teaching us what it means in daily practice.

For by one sacrifice he has made perfect forever those who are being made holy.

HEBREWS 10:14

The great transcendent God of all creation and glory calls us to come to Him and to accept that His yoke be placed upon us.

The humble, submissive Son of God, in complete obedience to His Father, shows us the way to come and to accept to be yoked to Him so that we may learn of Him.

The whole tenor of the teaching of the Holy Spirit through the Scriptures is an appeal to us to renounce our own stubborn wills and to submit to God's 'good, pleasing and perfect will', taking God at His word and coming to Him in glad acceptance of His yoke, which, being placed upon us, will enable us to learn of Him.

I will instruct you and teach you in the way you should go; I will counsel you with my loving eye on you. Do not be like the horse or the mule, which have no understanding but must be controlled by bit and bridle or they will not come to you.

PSALM 32:8-9

Why do we need to submit to the yoke?

Submission is essential if we are to fulfil the destiny for which we were created. We were created in the mind of God before He had even laid the foundation of the world, to be 'containers'. Containers need to be filled, if they are to function. God's plan was that we should be filled with His Holy Spirit and so reveal godliness. This demands that we agree to be emptied of self first, so as to be filled with Him. That is the essence of submission, replacing the self with the Christ, replacing my will with His will.

Therefore do not be foolish, but understand what the Lord's will is. Do not get drunk on wine, which leads to debauchery. Instead, be filled with the Spirit.

EPHESIANS 5:17-18

We are actually invited to be the home of God Himself. A temple, despite all possible ornate glory in its construction, despite all pain and varnish on its exterior, all carving and carpeting in its interior, is meaningless and unable to function if its doors are padlocked and no one allowed to enter or to worship there. As God's temples, we are created to be lived in, indwelt by God. Time and again in the Scriptures, God has promised to be our God and to live in our midst: 'I will live with them and walk among them, and I will be their God and they will be my people' (2 Cor. 6:16). 'If anyone loves me, he will obey my teaching. My Father will love him, and we will come to him and make our home with him' (John 14:23); and it is His presence that makes our temples worthy of their existence.

> *Do you not know that your bodies are temples of the Holy Spirit, who is in you, whom you have received from God? You are not your own; you were bought at a price. Therefore honour God with your bodies.*
>
> 1 CORINTHIANS 6:19-20

The Church is to be considered as Christ's Body, and we are all members of that Body: fingers, hands, arms; toes, feet, legs; eyes and ears, lips and mouths. A finger apart from a body has no meaning, no life, no usefulness. Lips without a head to command their manner of speech cannot function as they were designed to do. We need to be part of Him, to have His life-force coursing through our blood vessels, controlling our nervous impulses, directing our actions and reactions, to enable us to fulfil the meaning of our existence.

Now you are the body of Christ,
and each one of you is a part of it.

1 CORINTHIANS 12:27

Our Lord Jesus Christ Himself called us 'branches' and Himself the Vine: 'I am the vine; you are the branches. If a man remains in me and I in him, he will bear much fruit; apart from me you can do nothing' (John 15:5).

A branch, cut off from the trunk, withers and dies and is cast out to be burned. It is useless. It cannot bear fruit and, if dried and warped, it cannot be used for building or for carving. It has no strength nor life apart from the living sap that it should contain.

If anyone does not remain in me, he is like a branch that is thrown away and withers; such branches are picked up, thrown into the fire and burned. If you remain in me and my words remain in you, ask whatever you wish, and it will be done for you.

JOHN 15:6-7

Submission is the only way we have to express our love for God. God created us in His own image, to be to the praise of His glory, and to worship, *love*, and serve Him. In the Garden of Eden, God gave man everything he needed to live in happiness and harmony with Himself. He surrounded man with all the beauty of His creation. But as God wanted His creatures to love Him, He had to give them the ability to choose to do so. Love that is obligatory is not love. A robot cannot love because it cannot choose, and the very essence of love is that the lover chooses to love.

You will seek me and find me when
you seek me with all your heart.

JER. 29:13

God does not insist or force. He does not subject me to His laws. He loves me so deeply that He trusts me with the gift of free will so that I have the ability to choose to love and so to obey Him. He says: 'Whoever has my commands and obeys them, he is the one who loves Me… If anyone loves me, he will obey my teaching' (John 14:21-3).

Throughout the Scriptures, obedience is given as the one way pleasing to our Creator God by which we can express to Him our love, and such obedience always demonstrates the submission of my will to His.

To obey is better than sacrifice,
   and to heed is better than the fat of rams
(1 Sam. 15:22).

But thanks be to God that, though you used to be slaves to sin, you have come to obey from your heart the pattern of teaching that has now claimed your allegiance.

ROMANS 6:17

If I submit to the devil and myself, I am under the domination of sin, which leads me to spiritual death. But if I submit to the authority of God, I am under His dominion, which leads me to eternal life. 'Though you used to be slaves to sin, you wholeheartedly obeyed the form of teaching to which you were entrusted. You have been set free from sin and have become slaves to righteousness' (Rom. 6:17-18). To obey wholeheartedly is to give voluntary submission to Christ.

But now that you have been set free from sin and have become slaves of God, the benefit you reap leads to holiness, and the result is eternal life.

ROMANS 6:22

How we all long for that deep rest of heart and mind that only God can give! Jesus promised to give His disciples His peace – unmeasured, infinite, constant, unchanging peace. Peace that will replace the pressures and near-panic and utter weariness that fill so many of us as we labour in our service for God. He meant us to have peace, to be at rest in Him. He never intended that we should be overwhelmed and almost shattered by the vastness of the task to which we are called as His ambassadors. But so often we choose to shoulder the load alone, refusing to submit to Him, refusing to surrender our right to be loners and so refusing to roll the load back on to Him, who is waiting to receive it.

Come to me, all you who are weary and burdened, and I will give you rest.

MATTHEW 11:28

Why do we resist so strongly His patient invitation to submit and accept? 'Take my yoke upon you and learn from me' (Matt. 11:29).

It is as though the Almighty pleads with each one of us in turn, 'I'll be so patient and kind with you. I will lend you all My strength and give you My power. I'll carry the heavy end of the burden. I'll only place on you the little bit that I know you can manage. I'll help you over the rough places and lead you where there is green pasture and running water for your refreshment. I want you to learn to live My way, to think My way, to love My way; and I am willing to teach you everything that pleases Me.'

The LORD is my shepherd, I lack nothing.
He makes me lie down in green pastures, he leads me
beside quiet waters, he refreshes my soul.

PSALM 23:1-3

Sometimes the way of obedience may seem very humdrum, ordinary and unexciting – and we could easily think up all sorts of devices and gimmicks to cheer it all up… but God has His own perfect plan, and all He asks of us is submissive obedience to Him in love.

When we submit and bend our necks under His yoke, we find His yoke is smooth. It fits us exactly, with no chafing. It makes us want to pull and go with Him. As we break our proud wills and submit in obedience to His gentle will, work becomes a joy instead of drudgery:

The sacrifices of God are a broken spirit;
A broken and contrite heart,
O God, you will not despise.
(Ps. 51:17)

For this is what the high and lofty One says –
he who lives for ever, whose name is holy:
'I live in a high and holy place,
but also with him who is contrite and lowly in spirit,
to revive the spirit of the lowly
and to revive the heart of the contrite.'
(Isa. 57:15)

Return to the LORD your God, for he is gracious and compassionate, slow to anger and abounding in love, and he relents from sending calamity.

JOEL 2:13

Am I, are you, living our daily lives in perfect submission to His will? My relationship to God, as an adopted child through the shed blood of Calvary, demands that I submit happily and willingly to Him as my Father as well as my Creator. Have I yielded myself to Him as His love-slave? Will I do so daily through the rest of my life? Only thus can we go out to serve Him in the power of the Spirit.

It is here that we must start. We cannot rightly relate to and therefore have FELLOWSHIP with our fellow-men if we have not submitted to God's rightful authority over us. Once this submission to the yoke of Christ is fully established in my heart and life, then I can seek to bring others to Him. Our service *for* Christ, as we shall see in subsequent chapters, depends on our submission *to* Christ. We must accept the *yoke* before we can use the *towel*.

The Spirit you received does not make you slaves, so that you live in fear again; rather, the Spirit you received brought about your adoption to sonship. And by him we cry, 'Abba, Father.'

ROMANS 8:15

Jesus came to serve His Father by revealing Him and His character through His obedience and self-expending love. There is no greater service that anyone can give to another than to reveal the character of the one served by the service rendered. 'No one has ever seen God, but the only begotten Son, who is at the Father's side, has made him known' (John 1:18) From eternity, the Word was and is and ever will be a Servant.

The Lord Jesus Christ was *God*, and yet He served God in creating all that was made, in giving life to all beings, and by shining light into our darkness. 'God… has spoken to us by his Son, whom he appointed heir of all things, and through whom he made the universe' (Heb. 1:1-2).

This service that you perform is not only supplying the needs of the Lord's people but is also overflowing in many expressions of thanks to God.

2 CORINTHIANS 9:12

He came to us to 'communicate' God. Within the limitations of our humanity, He came to make the Godhead real to our human understanding. The Word was the expression of the whole Godhead in all its fullness. As such, He came to us to serve us – and we despised and rejected Him. We scorned God's Message to us, Who was the very Son of God.

Who has believed our message
*   and to whom has the arm of the Lord been revealed?…*
He was despised and rejected by men,
*   a man of sorrows, and familiar with suffering.*
Like one from whom men hide their faces
*   he was despised, and we esteemed him not.*
(Isa. 53:1, 3)

All things have been committed to me by my Father. No one knows who the Son is except the Father, and no one knows who the Father is except the Son and those to whom the Son chooses to reveal him.

LUKE 10:22

He, the Servant-Word, revealed God to us in all His grace and mercy, love and forbearance, in that He veiled His glory in the manger-birth that we might see Him; in that He forgave our sins when we sought only physical healing; in that He stilled the storm when our hearts failed us for fear; and supremely in that He died for us when we were yet His enemies, when outpoured love became the vanquisher of the last enemy, death. This tender Lover of our souls longs for our service, having prepared good works for us to do from the foundation of the world, even as He planned our redemption.

For we are God's handiwork, created in Christ Jesus to do good works, which God prepared in advance for us to do.

EPHESIANS 2:10

He, the Servant-Word, revealed God to us in all His truth and holiness, purity and righteousness: through all His teaching and ministry; through all His sinless life; even through His wrath at the desecration of the Temple by commercial greed; and supremely on the Cross, when He became sin that we might become the righteousness of God in Him, when God the Father turned away His eyes, being of purer eyes than to behold iniquity, and when that despairing cry was wrung from His lips, 'My God, My God, why have you forsaken me?' (Matt. 27:46).

However, as it is written: 'No eye has seen, no ear has heard, no mind has conceived what God has prepared for those who love him' – but God has revealed it to us by his Spirit.

1 CORINTHIANS 2:9-10

And in serving us, the Word was spent. He gave 'his life as a ransom for many' (Mark 10:45).

He was always giving. When, from within the massing crowd, the woman who had been ill for many years touched Him, He knew He had been 'touched' with purpose. How did He know? He Himself tells us, 'Power has gone out from me' (Luke 8:46).

He felt divine strength going out from Him as He served this woman at the point of her need. He was always being spent on our behalf. When He had walked from Jerusalem northwards towards Galilee, and had come to Jacob's well, near to the city of Sychar, we read: 'Jesus, tired as he was from the journey, sat down by the well' (John 4:6), in order that He might meet with the lonely outcast woman who came at midday to fill her water-pots; spent that she might be satisfied. On the Cross He cried out, 'I thirst'; spent that we might be satisfied.

God made him who had no sin to be sin for us, so that in him we might become the righteousness of God.

2 CORINTHIANS 5:21

God knew that His Son would be born of a virgin (Isa. 7:14), in the town of Bethlehem (Mic. 5:2), that He would grow up, 'like a tender shoot, and like a root out of dry ground' (Isa. 53:2), chosen of His Father though despised by men. The Son declared through the writings of the prophet:

I offered my back to those who beat me,
  my cheeks to those who pulled out my beard;
I did not hide my face
  from mocking and spitting
(Isa. 50:6).

God knew from the beginning of time that His Son must suffer – suffer humiliation at the hands of wicked men, be taken and abused, falsely accused and denied justice, flogged, scorned, spat upon – if men were to be redeemed, if men were to be reconciled to their Maker. And with a breaking heart, out of a love incomprehensible to the selfish soul of man, God planned the suffering of His Son that we might be adopted into His family as co-heirs with Christ:

See, my servant…
Surely he took up our infirmities
  and carried our sorrows,
yet we considered him stricken by God,
  smitten by him, and afflicted.
But he was pierced for our transgressions,
  he was crushed for our iniquities;
the punishment that brought us peace
  was upon him,

and by his wounds we are healed.
We all, like sheep, have gone astray,
each of us has turned to his own way;
and the LORD has laid on him
  the iniquity of us all
(Isa. 52:13, 53:4-6).

Now if we are children, then we are heirs –heirs
of God and co-heirs with Christ, if indeed we
share in his sufferings in order that we may
also share in his glory.

ROMANS 8:17

As *Son of Man*, He constantly submitted Himself to His Father's loving purpose – the salvation of sinners. All else had to be subordinate. It was indeed for this that His Father sent Him into the world – that we might be saved from the consequence of our sin. To redeem us from eternal death, separation from Almighty God, the Lord Jesus Christ steadfastly set His face to go up to Jerusalem, even though He knew, without doubt, that He must 'suffer many things at the hands of the elders, chief priests and teachers of the law and … be killed' (Matt. 16:21).

For this reason he had to be made like his brothers in every way, in order that he might become a merciful and faithful high priest in service to God, and that he might make atonement for the sins of the people.

HEBREWS 2:17

Let us pause and ponder on those three dreadful hours on the Cross. Even nature hid her eyes as darkness covered the earth. The morbid curiosity, the stark antagonism, the resentful jealousy, the puzzled misunderstanding, the brokenhearted love, the desperate need – all emotions were stilled and silenced. His yearning prayer, breathed over that watching crowd, 'Father, forgive them, for they do not know what they are doing' (Luke 23:34), must have caused a wave of unbelief, if not of guilt, as His attitude of acceptance proved so different from that usually shown by others. Then this last great cry of triumph rang out, 'It is finished,' and the Saviour, the perfected Saviour, 'bowed his head and gave up his spirit' (John 19:30).

There on the Cross, the Son of Man died an absolute death to self in every form; He demonstrated a complete submission to His heavenly Father's will and love; He finished that which was necessary for a total salvation and remission of sins and restoration into FELLOWSHIP for sinners.

But God demonstrates his own love for us in this:
While we were still sinners, Christ died for us.

ROMANS 5:8

As our Servant, Christ exemplified submission to His Father's will. He told us so clearly that He was among us as 'one who serves' (Luke 22:27). We know that He went about 'doing good' (Acts 10:38). His whole life demonstrates to us a selflessness and self-giving for others that could only be possible as the result of submission to the Father. His self-life was completely swallowed up in His desire and compassion towards others. He had no limit to what He would give for others – time, strength, love, caring – even to the extent of having no time so much as to eat. 'We must do the work of him who sent me' (John 9:4). Always His one concern was to fulfil His Father's purpose: the foundational reason for the Word being made flesh and dwelling among men.

> *This was to fulfill what was spoken through the prophet Isaiah: 'Here is my servant whom I have chosen, the one I love, in whom I delight; I will put my Spirit on him, and he will proclaim justice to the nations.'*
>
> MATTHEW 12:17-19

Humility is an attitude of life that is made possible to us as we yield unreservedly to the Saviour. 'Christ in you, the hope of glory' (Col. 1:27).

How can that be? It comes about in practical experience as I submit to God. I have to learn to be submissive not just in the big and dramatic things when everyone is watching – that is not particularly difficult! – but in the little, unspectacular things as well. When God asks me to serve in the background, to be unnoticed and unthanked, to be willing to be considered a fool for His sake, how do I react? And it is not only when the world ridicules me (I should expect that), but if it is fellow-Christians (whom I feel should know better) who do the ridiculing – or even close and dear friends, who just seem unable to understand – how do I react then?

Who is wise and understanding among you?
Let them show it by their good life, by deeds
done in the humility that comes from wisdom.

JAMES 3:13

As we gaze on the Lamb of God and allow Him to empty us of ourselves and fill us with Himself, Christ's humility will take over and replace our pride.

Such submission to God may be interpreted by the world as failure. There will be no loud acclaim for acts undertaken in that attitude of heart; there may be no visible fruit for service given with the one desire of glorifying the Father, rather than ourselves. 'Except a corn of wheat fall into the ground and die...' (John 12:24, KJV).

Is that what I want – to be ignored, forgotten, despised? Death to all that the world holds precious – acclaim, recognition, reward? Fruit only results from the death of the seed. So long as the seed hangs on to life in itself, there will be no fruit. But if it dies, it will not be conscious of the fruit! Is that what I seek? Do I so long for spiritual fruit from my ministry, that I will embrace death to self that it may be achieved? 'What you sow does not come to life unless it dies' (1 Cor. 15:36).

And I pray that you, being rooted and established in love, may have power, together with all the Lord's holy people, to grasp how wide and long and high and deep is the love of Christ, and to know this love that surpasses knowledge – that you may be filled to the measure of all the fullness of God.

EPHESIANS 3:17-19

Service completes us. Service gives meaning to our existence. By serving, we can be fulfilled: we can find our purpose in life. An exquisitely carved crystal vase may be an object of great intrinsic beauty, but if it is considered as a container, it is not fulfilling its function while it stands empty. To be filled with clean water and to carry a colourful display of flowers would fulfil its function of containing. A life lived to show off its own beauty, abilities and/ or independence may attract to itself, but will not fulfil the function for which God created it. God created us to contain the Holy Spirit that He might show forth the fruit of Christianity in service to others.

Each of you should use whatever gift you have received to serve others, as faithful stewards of God's grace in its various forms.

1 PETER 4:10

God created us to be givers, not getters. The world says, 'What can I get out of it? Where do I come in? What gain is there for *me* if I get involved in this?' but God gives and gives and goes on giving. He is the eternal Giver. He gave His Son that we might be forgiven. 'For God so loved the world that he gave…' (John 3:16).

God has shown us all through the Scriptures that giving is the tangible and real expression of love, and giving is the root of service. We are to give ourselves in service for others if we are to be Christlike and to act in accordance with God's plan for our lives. All the time we think in terms of 'getting' – receiving esteem, being in the limelight, gaining in popularity, building up our personal reputation – we are failing to fulfil God's purpose for us, which is that we should be givers.

> *Remember this: Whoever sows sparingly will also reap sparingly, and whoever sows generously will also reap generously. Each of you should give what you have decided in your heart to give, not reluctantly or under compulsion, for God loves a cheerful giver.*
>
> 2 CORINTHIANS 9:6-7

There was never a barrier between Jesus and people. He was always willing for interruptions: He almost seemed to welcome them! Having crossed the Sea of Galilee to have a quiet day with His disciples, apart from the constant pressure of the crowds, He 'saw a large crowd' who had foot-slogged all through the night, right round the lake, in order to hear more of His teaching. Immediately, with no thought of His own weariness or plan for the day, we read that, 'He had compassion on them, because they were like sheep without a shepherd' (Mark 6:34). He gave up His right to a day of peace and quiet, for rest and personal refreshment, and 'began teaching them many things'. As the day passed and evening approached, He went the second mile and provided them all with physical sustenance before sending them homewards! It was a severe interruption to His own desired programme, but He behaved in such a way, that 5,000 people felt welcomed and wanted.

You, my brothers and sisters, were called to be free. But do not use your freedom to indulge the flesh; rather, serve one another humbly in love.

GALATIANS 5:13

Then, too, Jesus washed Judas' feet, realising that only He knew what was in the heart of Judas and what he was about to do. Therefore He didn't do it in order that they might all think how wonderful He was to be so generous and forgiving in spirit. Jesus' service to Judas was just the same as He was rendering to the rest. Some of us have to be seen to be serving before we'll serve. We need the applause of people, saying how gracious or generous or public-spirited we are, before we'll act. We want people to know who it was that did the service, even if they did not actually see it being done, so that we do not lose the praise. Jesus worked even when there was no praise.

> *But when you give to the needy, do not let your left hand know what your right hand is doing, so that your giving may be in secret. Then your Father, who sees what is done in secret, will reward you.*
>
> MATTHEW 6:3-4

When we, as Christians, are 'complete in the Lord Jesus Christ', others around us will be able to see, hear and sense Him through us, even if they do not notice or remember us. It is essential that we are not such strong personalities that we block their view of the Master. If we would serve them, it must be as pointers to the Saviour, 'Let your light shine before men, that they may see your good deeds and praise your Father in heaven' (Matt. 5:16). Those around us are not meant to be drawn to us to glorify ourselves and so to increase our ego, but to be drawn to our Saviour and to glorify our heavenly Father. It should be for us as it was for John the Baptist, 'He [the Lord Jesus Christ] must become greater; I must become less' (John 3:30).

But if anyone obeys his word, God's love is truly made complete in him. This is how we know we are in him: Whoever claims to live in him must walk as Jesus did.

1 JOHN 2:5-6

God wants, above all else, that we should worship Him. He prepared ways for that worship that were pleasing and acceptable to Himself. He gave Moses a wonderful and detailed vision of the Tabernacle, 'the tent of Meeting', and Moses had it made and erected 'according to the pattern shown [him] on the mountain' (Exod. 25:40). God then gave Moses a detailed explanation as to how men were to approach Him in that Tabernacle in order to worship Him in a worthy manner. No one was to approach Him without the offering of a blood sacrifice, and the animal offered was to be without blemish. With amazing detail, reflecting all the varying aspects and meaning of the sacrifice of His Son on Calvary, the different offerings were instituted.

Besides all of which, there were regulations for transporting the Tabernacle from place to place when the campsite was moved. There were detailed laws given as to how it was to be dismantled, carried and re-erected in the next campsite. All this ceremonial was to ensure that the worship of the people would be acceptable to God.

Ascribe to the LORD the glory due his name.
Bring an offering and come before him; worship
the LORD in the splendour of his holiness.

1 CHRONICLES 16:29

We were created to love and worship God, and therefore given our free will to enable us to choose to do so. God wishes to pour into us His love – for we love Him 'because He first loved us' (1 John 4:19) – so that we have wherewith to love Him! But if we are to receive His love in order to love Him and those around us, we have to reckon with the fact that it was His love for us that drove Him to suffer. The very love He pours into us is a love that suffers. We have to be willing and prepared to suffer if we would embrace His love. True love always leads to suffering: there is no escape. Only where men do not love, can they hope not to suffer.

For just as we share abundantly in the sufferings of Christ, so also our comfort abounds through Christ.

2 Corinthians 1:5

ALSO AVAILABLE
IN THE 'LIVING' SERIES ...

Living Holiness

Willing to be the Legs of a Galloping Horse

Helen Roseveare

Drawing from her many years of experience as a doctor in Zaire, Dr. Roseveare vividly illustrates her own personal journey toward the holiness of God. She has faced many disappointments on the way through her own lack of Christlikeness – and failures to live up to God's standards of righteousness.

With deep humility, she shares with the reader her faltering steps in the process of learning what it means to be holy as God is holy.

978-1-8455-0352-9

DR. HELEN ROSEVEARE

"Each time I read one of her accounts, I want
to be like her. I want to know God as she does."
Noël Piper

LIVING
SACRIFICE
**WILLING TO BE
WHITTLED AS
AN ARROW**

Living Sacrifice
Willing to be Whittled as an Arrow
Helen Roseveare

What place does 'Sacrifice' have in the modern world? The Bible says it is central – and that sacrifice is not only a vital key to the future, it is the essence of a Christian's life, today. Helen Roseveare skilfully weaves stories of sacrifice together with Christian teaching on the subject to show you how Sacrifice is the key to joy.

978-1-8455-0294-2

Living Faith

Willing to be Stirred as a Pot of Paint

Helen Roseveare

'The quiet, consistent lives of Christian students drew me and began to convince me… They talked of faith as an objective reality, not a blind leap-in-the-dark, hoping for the best … They spoke of faith as a fact, a gift from God Himself to His people to enable them to grasp and comprehend truth.'

Thus starts Helen Roseveare's search for spiritual understanding of the world around her – a world on which she was to have a significant impact once her new faith led her to Africa.

978-1-8455-0295-9

Living Fellowship
Willing to be the Third Side of the Triangle
Helen Roseveare

'God is the hub of our wheel', states Helen Roseveare, 'and we are the spokes reaching out to the rim of the world.' *Living Fellowship* examines the true meaning of biblical communion as a dynamic relationship between God, ourselves and others. True fellowship will involve submission, service, and suffering. Taking each theme in turn, Helen Roseveare draws on the teaching of Scripture and personal experience to show the practical outworking of God's invitation to us to share in a relationship with Him.

978-1-8455-0351-2

Christian Focus Publications

Our mission statement –

STAYING FAITHFUL

In dependence upon God we seek to impact the world through literature faithful to His infallible Word, the Bible. Our aim is to ensure that the Lord Jesus Christ is presented as the only hope to obtain forgiveness of sin, live a useful life and look forward to heaven with Him.

Our Books are published in four imprints:

CHRISTIAN
FOCUS

popular works including biographies, commentaries, basic doctrine and Christian living.

CHRISTIAN
HERITAGE

books representing some of the best material from the rich heritage of the church.

MENTOR

books written at a level suitable for Bible College and seminary students, pastors, and other serious readers. The imprint includes commentaries, doctrinal studies, examination of current issues and church history.

CF4•K

children's books for quality Bible teaching and for all age groups: Sunday school curriculum, puzzle and activity books; personal and family devotional titles, biographies and inspirational stories – because you are never too young to know Jesus!

Christian Focus Publications Ltd,
Geanies House, Fearn, Ross-shire,
IV20 1TW, Scotland, United Kingdom.
www.christianfocus.com